IT HAPPENED IN THE KITCHEN

RECIPES FOR FOOD AND THOUGHT

ROSE B. NADER

AND

NATHRA NADER

Published by:

Center for Study of Responsive Law
P.O. Box 19367
Washington, DC 20036   Price $9.00

Library of Congress Catalog Card Number: 91-70432

ISBN # 0-936758-29-5
Printed in the United States of America.

Dedicated
to
Shafeek Nader

ACKNOWLEDGMENTS

This volume is a result of Operation Cooperation. We thank our children, Claire, Laura and Ralph, and Shafeek who throughout his life cared deeply about family and community; family and friends who have sat around our table for food and thought; the people in communities where I have lived and through whom I had the life experiences that taught me so much; my own parents and sisters who provided the first settings for these experiences; my wonderful grandchildren, Nadia, Tarek and Rania who listen and who relished the food I prepared for them, and then paid me a compliment by making some of the various dishes presented here.

I thank Joan Claybrook for her enthusiastic assistance, Hays Gorey for his early recognition, and Beverly Orr, John Richard and Amy Allina for their technical help in preparing the manuscript for publication.

R.B.N.

CONTENTS

ACKNOWLEDGMENTS

PREFACE 9

PART ONE ~ *Food for Thought by Rose B. Nader* 13

PART TWO ~ *The Food* 39

Helpful Hints For the Recipes 39

APPETIZERS 43
   Hummus bi Tahini (Chick Peas with Sesame Seed Paste) 44
   Baba Ghanoogh (Eggplant with Sesame Seed Paste) 46
   Salmon 47
   Chicken Spread 48

SOUPS 49
   Lamb Broth 50
   Lamb Broth Soup 51
   Blackeyed Pea Soup 52
   Lentil-Soybean Soup 53
   Cucumbers with Laban 54

SALADS 55
   Tabouli (Parsley, Scallions and Tomatoes with Burghul) 56
   Fatoosh (Tomatoes, Scallions and Parsley with Toasted Bread) 57
   Potato Salad 58
   Salata (Tossed Salad) 59
   Swiss Chard Salad 60

MAIN DISHES WITH MEAT 61
   Shaykh il Mihshee (Baked Eggplant Stuffed with Lamb & Pine Nuts) 62
   Sfeeha or Fatayer (Open-Faced or Stuffed Pastry with Lamb) 64
   Dough for Sfeeha or Fatayer 66
   Shishbarak (Stuffed Bread Dough in Labaneeye or Kishk) 67
   Kibbi (Ground Lamb with Wheat Grain) 68
   Filling for Kibbi and Baked Kibbi 69
   Kibbi Patties Broiled (Kibbi Mishweeye) 71

Stuffed Kibbi 71
Stuffed Kibbi Cooked in Labaneeye (Yogurt) or Kishk 72
Kibbi in Tomato Sauce 73
Kibbi with Kishk and Vegetables 74
Chicken with Lamb and Rice (Dajaje ma'a Hashwee) 75
Chicken in Casserole 77
Roast Turkey 78
Lamb Stew with Lima or String Beans (Yakhnat Loubieh) 79
Baked Okra with Lamb (Bamieh ma'a Lahm) 80
Eggplant Stew (Yakhnat Beitinjan) 81
Lamb Patties with Spinach (Kaftas ma'a Yakhnat Sabaneeckh) 82
Zucchini Stuffed with Lamb and Rice (Koosa Mihshee) 84
Rolled Stuffed Grape Leaves (Yabrak Arish) 86
Rolled Stuffed Cabbage (Yabrak Malfoof) 88
Zucchini or Summer Squash with Lamb (Koosa ma'a Lahm) 89
Ablama 90
Lamb with Asparagus 91
Lamb Kaftas (Patties) with Vegetables 92
Beef Kaftas (Patties) with Peas 94
Beef with Wine 95
Burghul Falfal (Ground Lamb and Cracked Wheat) 96
Stuffed Potatoes 97

MAIN DISHES WITH VEGETABLES 99
Vegetable Casserole 100
Burghul with Swiss Chard or Chicory Lettuce 101
Blackeyed Peas 102
'Mdardara (Lentils with Rice and Scallions) 103
'Mjadara (Lentils with Rice and Onions) 104
Rolled Grape Leaves with Chick Peas 105
Baked Squash Omelet 106
Rice with Zucchini 107
Kibbi with Potatoes (Kibbit Batata) 108
Chick Peas and Laban on Toast 109

MAIN DISHES WITH FISH 111
Fish with Vegetables 112
Baked Fish with Spices and Tarator Sauce 113
Fish with Wheat Grain (Kibbit Samak) 114

VEGETABLES 115
   String Beans with Olive Oil (Loubieh bi Zayt) 116
   Eggplant with Lemon, Olive Oil and Garlic 117
   Beet Leaves or Swiss Chard with Olive Oil and Onions 118
   Beets with Onion and Olive Oil 119
   Steamed Broccoli with Garlic, Lemon and Olive Oil 119
   Steamed Cauliflower with Tarator Sauce 120
   Fava Beans with Olive Oil (Foole) 120

DESSERTS 121
   Ma'mool (Pastry filled with Crushed Pistachio Nuts) 122
   Macaroon Kashab (Glazed Sesame Seed Macaroon) 124
   Namoura 126
   Ka'ak (A Sweet Yeast Bread) 127
   Stuffed Honey Dew 128
   Halawa bi Jibney (Sweet Cheese Pudding) 129
   Parfait 130
   Cream Cheese Gelatin Delight 131
   Apple Cake 132
   Cranberry with Oranges and Apples 134
   Christmas Bread 135
   Rice Pudding 136
   Two-Two-Two Cookies 137
   Oatmeal Cookies 138
   Coconut, Walnut and Raisin Cookies 139
   Sesame Seed Coconut Cookies 140
   Date Nut and Sesame Seed Cookies 141
   Carrot Coconut Cookies 142

SOME BASICS 143
   Bread 144
   Rice 146
   Laban (Yogurt) 147
   Labaney 148
   Jibney (Cheese) 149

PART THREE ~ *More Food for Thought from Nathra Nader* 151

PREFACE

We have all heard the term holistic medicine, but we do not think of the family, whatever its size and shape, in holistic terms. On the contrary, much has been written on the loss of functions of the family. I suppose it is this talk of loss that has stimulated people to write to me asking how I brought up my children, what we ate and talked about around the dinner table, and what advice I could give to them, parents and children. More than a few of these letters asked the question, "What did you feed Ralph Nader?" *It Happened in the Kitchen* uses food, its preparation, its consumption, its overall meaning for the individual, the family household, the neighborhood, and the community as an avenue to answering some of those questions.

Basically there are three parts to this book. In Part One will be found stories that reflect my thoughts about food, upbringing and other matters of importance. We all need to express our philosophies in an age where the family has lost so much of its power, in raising the next generation, to external influences, the streets, marketplaces and social service agencies. What is new and recent is not always better and for this reason it is important to reflect on what has been lost in order to recapture those joys of living within the family that easily spring from the culture of the kitchen.

Part Two presents the recipes I use most frequently. These recipes are kept simple. They are not overly detailed because my style is one of flexibility and using my own judgment. In some places I illustrate how I write recipes for my children and grandchildren in which I omit the precision found in many contemporary recipe books (such as 1/3 cup of sugar, when it could as well be ¼ or 1/8) because cooking is an art that should vary from one artist to another. Rather than being cast in stone, recipes that are general, like those I write for my family, allow the cook to play and invent. Precision is not as important as nutrition for example, and with experience I hope that these recipes are modified to fit the requirements of the cook. I should also note that this book is not about nutrition, although the recipes mostly do reflect basic nutritional guidelines. They are low in fat, high in fiber, low in sodium and offer a variety of foods. There is little need to count calories when this food is eaten in moderation.

The third part of this book is the children's recollections of their father's penetrating and ironic commentaries, collected over the years, at home with the children and in his restaurant business with friends and customers.

The interwoven format reflects the integrative nature of food and thought from home to community. Food is more than sustenance: it is an expression of health, affection, cultural transmission, stimulation, teaching, participation, and bonding. In our times, however, it has been disembodied. For the most part it is just considered fuel. Look at our homes and our kitchens throughout history. They were places of person-person interaction. Now they strike me as a person-machine interaction, the cook and the stove, the microwave oven, the refrigerator, the osterizer, electric knives, dishwashers, garbage disposals, often radio, television and computer. I sometimes think that loading a kitchen with so much machinery and implements turns claimed conveniences into a little used machine shop. A kitchen provides an atmosphere for human interaction, and while some modern appliances can be very useful, focusing on them can diminish the informality and familial associations over what, after all, should be relatively simple work with a few raw materials.

Overall, the thrust of the book is to trust in the ever-maturing value of your own judgment in place of a dependency on crutches of hyper-how-tos. I had at first thought to call this book *Use Your Own Judgment* because I think that creativity and confidence require it. By learning to use and expand your own judgment, it will grow and evolve far beyond the kitchen and family into the neighborhood and community as if to say, "My style in life is not introverted, but looks outward from a position of stability and nurturing onto the world to which I want to contribute." This integrated participation in life is the real significance of what happened in the kitchen as I was raising my family.

Rose B. Nader
January 1991

PART ONE

FOOD FOR THOUGHT
by
Rose B. Nader

My experience with family intimacy in the kitchen is as old as I am. My parents raised eight daughters, two nieces, and two nephews under one sod roof in the town of Zahle in Lebanon. The floors were tiled or cemented, and the memories of white walls, nomadic rugs, and kerosene lamps in that house bursting with people are vivid in my memory. We loved to laugh and laughed to love, and the kitchen was where it all happened. Preparing food, eating, and talking and laughing were all rolled into one cooperative effort, even under trying conditions of food shortages, epidemics and military occupations around the time of World War I.

It was in the kitchen that we learned about relatives who were not present, through life stories. There also was the daily recounting of happenings in the community; births and deaths, local politics, marriage and sickness, and the availability of food. While we ate and talked, stories would reveal the clash or triumphs of values. By the use of venerable proverbs our questions would be answered even before we asked: "The ignorant person learns at his own expense. The wise person at the expense of others." A political recounting might end with the proverb, "When your enemy is your judge, to whom do you complain?" Or, in referring to the availability of food, "If meat is expensive, patience is cheap." Or, in thinking about life problems, "When a man sees the other fellow's misfortunes, his own seem simple." And, always, there was the importance of family, "Though your own kinsmen may chew you, they will not swallow you."

When I was a child, my mother made almost everything from scratch, our clothes, our wool-filled mattresses, our food, and early on I tried to do the same because it gave me a feeling of confidence. There was a little structure separate from our house, a place where the mud brick oven was located for baking bread weekly or biweekly. The memory of bread-baking is strong with me still. My mother used to take the round Arabic bread, fill it with potato mashed with olive oil, roll it up, one for each child and off to play we would go, grasping it tightly in our hands. At supper, parents and children would all sit down to eat together.

Our childhood was just that, a childhood, a time for growing and learning, for being mischievous and curious, for picking vegetables in the garden that was planted below our house and fruit in the *kroum*, a vineyard in the hills above the Bekkaa Valley. Lebanon was a cross-roads and so were our life experiences. As a little child I attended a Russian school for the first grade. World War I had left many refugees including the Armenians, a large refugee group, some of whom helped with our vegetable garden. Turkish soldiers were coming around our neighborhood daily, and when after World War I, Turkish control was followed by the French Mandate, French became a second language for me. But what I remember more than the political events of my childhood was what we did in our daily lives, how our mother took old trousers to make stylish hats for her children, how the migrant worker gave birth before my very eyes without the presence of a doctor or midwife, and how my mother helped her deliver the baby. I remember the walks to the vineyards to collect grapes and figs, and the close calls at night because of bears in the vicinity of our tent, or because Turkish soldiers were patrolling, and my father's protective presence. For a short while, I attended a Catholic school, and although we were Christian Orthodox and not Catholic, once my curiosity moved me to stand in line for confession only to have the Sisters discover and punish me by locking me in the dining room which had plenty of wine, an experience in itself.

And I remember my father making up lotions for curing the unwanted blemishes of his eight daughters, and admonishing us always to behave properly in the presence of young men in the town. Family reputation was important; the quality of our futures was dependent on a good family name. And when my mother returned to her village of birth to visit her family for a longish period, the older children assumed responsibility for taking care of younger siblings and cousins under my father's guidance.

Six of eight daughters became teachers. At one point I had an opportunity to teach in a large village several hours from Zahle. It was considered very risky for a daughter to sleep other than under her parents' roof, but the money offered more than doubled my salary in Zahle, and I was adventurous and confident that I could handle the challenge. And challenge me the villagers did. Sporadically they tested my intelligence through examination; they tested my morals through temptation; and they tested my generosity. When they were satisfied, they gave me their respect.

This teaching assignment was my first experience in being away from home; I lived in a tiny room rented from a family. I remembered the words that my parents had taught me: "If you want to keep your friend neither borrow from him nor lend him," or "He who needs a thing badly is blind," or "The friend who does you no good is like the adversary who does you no harm." Proverbs are helpful guides in the absence of family and especially for a young person encountering new experiences and new environments. But also I saw this new experience as both interesting and humorous, and much of what happened in that village I later used as stories to teach and entertain my children while we were eating lunch or dinner.

For example, I was teaching in this village during the influenza epidemic. Most students in my class had influenza. And although the medical doctor told me not to visit my students because I would then also fall sick, I wanted to visit my students who had gotten ill. I found them in their homes lying on their mattresses stretched out on the floor, and I brought them water and talked to them. My mother was worried that I would become sick and told me to return home. I didn't want to for fear I would infect my family. Instead I ate plenty of garlic to strengthen my immunity and continued to visit everyone in my class.

At the end of that teaching appointment I was married, and left Lebanon with my husband to come to the United States. At first, it was difficult to adjust to a strange environment. My husband worked long hours in his business, I was in my late teens and although I had studied English, I could not speak the language very well. It was also difficult to learn English because I discovered that neighbors did not talk that frequently to one another, nor did people often visit one another spontaneously. After we moved to Winsted, I recall one night when the lights in our apartment building went out, everybody came out of their corners and met each other by accident. I asked, how do people in this Connecticut community meet each other, and I was told you have to join clubs to meet people. So I joined clubs, the Women's Club, the Methodist Church Women's Club, the Parent Teachers Association. But without clubs one didn't meet many people socially, and it was lonely at first.

I used to write my mother in Lebanon for advice. She would advise me about my life and about my pregnancies and about how to raise and feed the children. She used to send me good and loving letters. It was calming to have her tell me "You have to climb a ladder one step at a time." She had strong views on raising children. "Make your child cry a little now rather than cry later over him," meaning one should deal directly and immediately with misbehavior, not let it mount up to a large problem in adulthood. She used to help make things easy for me by telling me not to worry, not every ship has wind in its sails. I still have my mother's letters, reread them with enjoyment and continue to learn from them.

When we were quite young, my mother went down to Beirut and bought a different colored dish for each child. I remember each child kept the same dish, and we did not change the color given to us. My mother did this to make us happy and to add color to our table. Each child took turns setting the table and washing dishes. She put us to work. Mother was not supposed to do everything. My mother had a wonderful sense of humor and always kept us laughing. We had a reputation in the neighborhood and people used to say go and watch the twelve children at our house to see how they eat together in an orderly manner rather than each child eating haphazardly. There is a saying that the daughter comes out like the mother, and my mother and her mother were both strong women.

When my children were young, we had an older Lebanese woman who helped with the housework once a week. She also visited us every day after she had her supper. She sat in the kitchen while we were eating and sometimes she joined us. We paid for her work, but we also provided her with food and company for she was widowed, and she enjoyed talking with the children. The children liked having her, and she watched how I was bringing up the children, then spread her observations in the community.

Raising Children

Children are human beings who need to have very close attention and love at the same time. I always asked my children if they were happy after hearing about what they had been doing. They used to run home from school for their lunch in anticipation because I had started a story of saga length. Every day I would tell them part of the story, for about five or ten minutes, the rest to be continued the next day and unfolding over several weeks (and remembered for years to come.). When I was finished with the saga, I would tell them Jeha stories for a change. Jeha was a mythical town fool and the stories about him were both funny and instructive.

When my children were small, I also used to recite stories about heroes, because heroes provided good examples of strong character traits. For example, to teach the children that there are reasons and benefits to good behavior I would note, 'a person who practices telling the truth is likely to discover more of it.' Sometimes I recited the parts of plays I had been in as a student, plays such as Joan of Arc in which I had played Joan of Arc.

But that was for lunch. There were few stories at supper. At supper the children would talk about what happened at school, and I would ask them what the teacher taught them. If any of them complained about not doing well I told them to study harder, at night, not in the morning before school. I would say to them, 'do not blame anyone but yourselves. To have a high goal without work is to no avail.' I would use a proverb. For example, "If you teach me one letter I am in your debt," meaning they should respect the teacher for teaching them. Or, I would encourage them by saying 'determination is what puts your dreams on wheels.'

If a child wouldn't sit down and write a term paper, but fretted anxiously about the prospect, I would say to them, 'a sure way to prolong misery is to be able to endure it.'

When they told me about their little fights, I would recite a proverb, "If you attack someone it returns to you, so don't." I heard their complaints and shared their problems, trying with them to find a way to solve their problems. When my first daughter was skittish about water, I arranged for her to take swimming lessons at the YMCA. All of that talk happened in the kitchen.

While a teacher I remember that the school administrator sent me an unruly child who earlier had been sent home from school because he was so difficult. His parents came to me and said, "His bones belong to us but his flesh belongs to you, teach him." He wouldn't sit still, and would send love notes to a girl who could not stand him. I spoke firmly to him and then sent him to fill the water jug, giving him a responsible chore at school. He calmed down, and his parents thanked me. I believe that a teacher should teach and a mother should also teach, not just pass information from one to another. When my children used to complain about their teachers, I would say to them, 'I believe it's you,' and on the wall I hung a saying, "Success is found in the soul of you, and not in the realm of luck." Then, if necessary, I would call the teacher separately and discuss the matter. 'I believe it's you' also helped in dealing with pressure from their fellow students or friends.

So much is in the training. After my children ate their lunch or dinner with satisfaction, I used to give each of them a job to do, then not later, to clear the table, to wash the dishes and to sweep the floor while I am with them, talking sometimes serious talk mixed with funny stories and sometimes we talked about their personalities. I taught them never to put off doing work or leave it for someone else to do.

I believe in teaching through criticism mixed with teasing and joking, sometimes giving them nicknames like "slow car" when they were slow to get a job done, or I would cite the proverb "wait until the grass grows, oh mule," or I would compare them with known personalities, like Jeha or some well-defined character. This is almost the opposite of what many psychologists recommend today, but it is how my parents built character, and I did the same. I used to call it Operation Cooperation when we worked together and talked together, and I never let the children say they did their best, explaining to them that unless you know everything and can do everything, never say you've done your best. Just say that you are doing better.

We've taught our children to respect the culture of their parents and the best in the culture into which they were born. They often spoke Arabic at home and were encouraged to excel in English. Language meant communication. We admired Arabic poetry and quoted poetry to the children. We had long before read Shakespeare in Arabic and could discuss his work with them.

The responsibility for raising children belongs to the parents, not to the child. Children are clever. They watch their parents and can take advantage where they see weakness. If parents don't discipline, if parents are indecisive, children won't respect them. I do not mean that children are not to be heard. When my children would explain to me, I would sometimes find that they were right, but I also explained my position. A child has to know why no, or why yes, but they should not incessantly argue.

I didn't care how long the children took to clean the house. It was their duty to clean house with me. You train the children to work and you teach them what to eat. You must also find ways to make sure that the children appreciate all your help and support so they do not take you for granted with all that involves. Children don't appreciate what they have if they routinely expect things and know they can get more.

My advice to parents today is not to be afraid of their children. If children see that their parents are afraid of them, then they will increase their influence over their parents and thereby lose their moorings or anchor. Be reasonable, be patient. Don't coerce and don't bribe. If a child finds out that he gets a lot of attention if he doesn't eat, then he's going to make his parents jump through a hoop. I would not ask my child what they would like to eat because young children do not know what is good for them. They don't have to like what they eat, they just have to eat it. Parents should eat the same food; no double standard.

Parents are supposed to be in charge. An African anthropologist once told my daughter that this was a country where children are supposed to bring themselves up. I guess he was referring to latchkey children and the television set raising them without parents. I dressed eight-year-old Ralph in short pants because I believed he still was too young for long pants even though he and other boys thought it was being babyish to wear short pants. And when he would argue that the other children weren't wearing short pants, I would tell him, 'so, you're different, other children have their mothers and you have yours.' When the children convinced me that chocolate frosted birthday cakes were what all the other children had, I frosted the cake, but after the candles were blown out and before they cut into the cake, I removed the frosting. Some people might say I was severe, but it became a family joke.

Children should have a childhood, and younger children should look up to older children. In that way you don't have a problem with sibling rivalry. The little ones are like kids and they follow the billy goat leader. In the afternoon when I enjoyed my solitude and rested for an hour or so, the oldest was in charge. And the other three had to obey him. However, some times the younger children would rebel, which offered the opportunity to talk about what mattered to the children, and to me. My oldest child was a good example for his siblings, and he helped me teach the younger children.

The family should strive to be together because there is a strength in togetherness, weakness in separateness. We wanted our children to be equally developed and, of course, showed no favoritism. We tried to protect them from the many disruptive, distorting influences on the family from the outside. Parents of today are frightened because of street crime, drugs, television violence and other problems, but they should not be intimidated. There is a saying in Arabic, "He who does not harden his heart is unable to bring up his child properly."

My teaching was not done by lecturing or haranguing. It was mostly by indirection and few opportunities to teach were wasted. A regular reply to any display of overconfident behavior by the children was 'you'd better be a genius because you've clearly decided to stop learning.' If they had too little self-confidence I would say, 'too little self-confidence is like putting a brake on your brain. The world is already full of obstacles in your way; you don't need to make more.'

I have known some parents who allow their children to watch television while they are eating. Recent polls say the majority of Americans watch TV, read, work or do something else while eating. In my view this is very wrong. Why? Because children should talk with their parents at dinner. In this way we can build strong communication between parents and children, which is very important for creating a good relationship between children and their parents.

Conversation has become a lost art especially for the post-television generations, and, it appears, they have forgotten how to have conversations. Children become upset or unhappy often because their frame of reference is too small. Children, nowadays, spend too little time with adults, including their parents. Conversation helps create understanding, discipline and social skills among children that staring at television, hour after hour, cannot begin to match. For example, I liked to pose two seemingly contradictory maxims such as "Look before you leap" and "He who hesitates is lost," and ask the children to resolve the differences with examples from their experiences or readings. We had a good time. I used to say to the children, 'you never know where you will find yourselves, or what you will find on your plate in strange lands.' I told them the story of when I was teaching in the village and had found a fly in my dish. I put it to one side and ate what was on the plate so as not to embarass my hosts. I trained them to be flexible and accommodating to their hosts. Nowadays, children argue with their parents about not wanting this or that, and dominate the conversation at the table. When my youngest daughter went to do her anthropological field work in the mountains of southern Mexico, she benefitted from my words about preparing for the unexpected when eating in strange lands.

Children learn some of the most important lessons at the family table. I taught my children manners as part of a game at the table: 'As the ship goes out to sea I shovel my food away from me.' A rhyme is easy to remember. "He who takes too big a mouthful shall find it difficult to swallow" is a proverb that is applicable to more situations than manners and eating. The children learned you did not take or eat food before the guests were served. When they did, I just gave them a quick look of disapproval (what they came to call "the look"), and that stopped what they were doing. Such silent language avoided any humiliation in front of company. I would also use dining as occasions to teach respect for older people, pointing out that there is much to learn from older people if we listen carefully.

To parents who were complaining that their children were not thankful for what they (the parents) do for them I would say, parents should *not* expect expressions of gratitude from their children; respect will suffice and, as their children grow older and wiser, respect will include gratitude.

Mr. Nader often spoke politics at the table. His favorite topics as the children were growing up dealt with colonialism, with superior kinds of taxation that benefit the whole society, with the stifling of small business by big business, with education for citizenship and with the basic needs of our local community. He taught the children the difference between religious behavior and organized religion. He also made the most wonderful ice cream using fresh fruit, and the children and their cousins (ten in all) would line up for the first ice cream out of the machine.

As for me, as the children grew older, my stories changed from those transmitting proper values and family experience, to concerns over food and health, contaminants in the environment, the absence of attentiveness to children's welfare in this country, nuclear war, and local needs such as maintaining a *community* hospital. We taught the children to converse and to think about life, to question and challenge, even engaging them in little mock debates.

One day my husband and I were in the yard with the children. We started asking if they knew the price of eggs, of apples, of bananas, lettuce, et cetera. They usually had accurate answers. Then we asked them to put a price on the clean air that day, the sunshine, or the cool breeze, the songs of the birds and the shade of the trees. They were stumped. We wanted them to appreciate what cannot be priced that is so valuable and pleasurable, that is priceless in nature.

More stories about life's experiences add to the children's personality, and older people become an opportunity to bequeath experience. One time an elderly neighbor fell on the ice and broke her arm. She was unable to dress herself and needed help. I sent my daughter Laura to help her. She didn't want to go, and she cried, but she went anyway, and it increased her confidence in what she could do.

There are key moments when raising children. When the children were sick, I gave them their lessons on health. You can't have a more receptive time than when a child is in the midst of chicken pox, mumps, whooping cough, measles. I would gently tell them, 'if you have your health, you have everything. Without it you have nothing.' It was then that I spoke with the children about the importance of eating well, and the importance of having adequate rest and exercise. I would tell them that such advice is part of a style of living, and I practiced what I preached.

I always have done exercise everyday. I exercised with the children. I played ball with them. I would go sledding with them, and before bed would do my exercises with the children, and, to show them the way, I always had to be the most vigorous.

Nutritious Food

Nutritious is delicious. When it comes to eating food, you either put your brain in charge of your tongue or your tongue will control your brain. When urging grimacing children to eat a nutritious plate I would say, 'what do your tongues have against your lungs, heart, kidney, and liver?'

My interest in nutritious food originated years ago as I was growing up in Lebanon. I was about 10 years old, and I remember my interest was sparked because I wanted a healthy body, and especially a healthy face for which I cared a lot. Later, I began to read about nutritious food, and also health care as written about in medical books. Probably the doctors in my mother's family were an influence, but I developed my own style in life by being interested in health and food, and my wish was to get married and bring up my children on this basis. It is very important to pay attention to children from their infant years, nourishing their body and mind *togothor*. Actually, in the Arabic language, food and words of endearment are closely linked. So that one might say to a child, "How delicious you are," or "how digestible," or "how tasty," or "how tender" and so forth.

As I said earlier, because food is not just sustenance, there is a sense of creativity in its consumption. It is a way of communicating, a way of teaching. I always believed that food was not only for the body. Sometimes when you eat something which isn't nourishing, you feel irritated and you don't know why. It is the food, it is the atmosphere, it all goes together. I never fed my children hot dogs. I didn't *know* they were bad, it was just that I didn't know what was put in the hot dog, and I didn't trust something I didn't know about. Now I read about the decline in quality of the hot dog. Since 1945, fat has risen from 14 to 30 percent while protein has declined from 15 to 11 percent.

We eat green salad practically every day. I experiment with different ideas for variety, and surprise my family. I believe in very simple food for people like me, because I have other interests on my mind. The important point for me is that the meal be nourishing and contribute to a healthy body and mind. I know such meals can also be delicious; there is no contradiction. Women who work both inside and outside the home should not fuss over food. They need a diet that is made of harmless, hearty food, as in Marian Burros' cookbook, *Keep it Simple*. Making life simpler allows them to continue managing both jobs, and I would encourage them to pull in all the family members to Operation Cooperation.

Read John Thorne, the iconoclast publisher of the *Simple Cooking Series*, and of *Simple Cooking*, the Boston-based quarterly newsletter that advocates the pleasures of simple foods – oatmeal – for example. Fancy and expensive are not necessarily better.

Cooking does not need to be drudgery. I get my best ideas when I'm chopping and mincing, and after years in this country, I discovered easy ways to cook meals, as you can see in this book. But cooking was based on my style and philosophy. I never liked eating fattening food. As a result, I lean towards beans, vegetables and grains. My mother used more fat in cooking than I did. In earlier days, there was more physical exertion since there were no cars; people walked a lot and digestion was easier. So my mother could cook richer food, and would exercise fancy cooking skills. Because my interest is not solely in cooking alone, but in health, I see food as a basic recipe for health.

When I first came to this country, I found American store bread gummy and I could not understand why. I especially looked into the quality of flour. It took me almost one year to discover that the flour used to bake bread in the United States was processed to remove bran and nutritious germ, and I could not understand why they called it "refined" flour. It was of lesser quality than the flour of my childhood.

The way we think affects our eating, our talk, walk and every move we make. More people now are aware of nutritious food so they know more about what they are eating. Many Americans are dramatically changing their preferences in food. They have reduced their salt and fat consumption. My bread fits with these changing food preferences. I bake a simple bread, a combination of water or skim milk, organic whole wheat flour, and yeast. Sometimes I add some soy flour and wheat germ. Someone once said of my bread, "Eat this bread and you will never spread," because it is a nutritious bread and not fattening. My grandson bakes this bread very well now.

It is up to parents to develop healthy habits as a model for the children. How? As Marian Burros says, "Let variety and moderation be the guide." You can tell what foods will agree with you or not. For instance, when the doctor examines your heart, it does not mean he or she can prevent a heart attack. But you can decrease the chances of a heart attack sometimes by simple measures of diet and exercise. Poor diet, no exercise and disease go together.

Let us talk about meat and vegetables. Eating too much fatty meat increases the death rate, unlike vegetables. In our family we don't eat much meat. Our diet also includes fish and, if organic, chicken. We use less than 1 pound of lean meat to serve about six persons.

One day, years ago, I met a gentleman walking down the street whom I have known for many years. His son was a meat inspector for the state. He told me the federal government had to send out federal inspectors because it did not trust state inspectors to inspect properly. He also told me that when his son was inspecting meat, he used to inspect steers and find cancer in some parts of the carcass. The meat plant would cut out the cancerous part and allow the rest to be sold. Can you imagine these sick meats being consumed by human beings? I asked if his son ate much meat and he said his son was a vegetarian.

I will stick to healthy vegetables, fruits and grains. There is protein in nuts, beans and lentils which we eat weekly and enjoy, and a banana daily provides me with the potassium I need.

They have long fed soybeans to livestock. Now many people in

Western countries (as well as in Eastern cultures) include soybeans in their own diet. You don't need to eat a lot at all; they are quite gassy.

I love to serve soup before meals, especially in wintertime. In the summer, I use laban (yogurt) which I always make from scratch. Commercial yogurt is a far cry from home-made laban in terms of flavor and texture. I try new things with laban. I never thought I could blend laban and tomato juice until recently and so I tried another variation with orange juice and mint leaves. It came out very tasty. Try it and see how you like it.

Ralph tells me I was ahead of my time because I avoided hot dogs, bologna, canned foods, white bleached bread, fatty meat, and because I emphasized fresh fruits and vegetables, and whole grains, high fiber foods, lean meat, homemade soups not canned soup. People's tastes are changing now; more people are eating hummus, tabouli, and laban (yogurt). Common sense sometimes precedes nutritional science.

Children and Their Imagination

It is mistaken to favor one child over another. Favoritism creates withdrawal, distance, sadness, and divisiveness. We wanted all our children to attend college so that they could share stimulating experiences.

Children often ask their parents which child do they like best. Instead of answering this question directly, I would tell them what the Bedouin mother answered when asked the question, "Which child do you like best?" The Bedouin answered, "I like the one who is farthest until they are near, the youngest until they grow older and the sick until they are well." By answering in this way the child learns that their question is not unusual, and it teaches them the wisdom of people who have not been formally schooled. It makes them think about more than themselves.

I always believe that children should learn how to use their imagination. When my children were small, I never bought them a doll or a game. They grew up mostly without such things. I told them stories or I read them stories, some of which they told to each other. My daughter did this with her children, and my oldest granddaughter invented stories for her brother and sister at least as long as they slept in the same room. She also organized them to put on skits of their imagination. I preferred telling stories to my children rather than reading to them because I could watch better their reactions, encourage their imagination, and teach them, keeping the exchange going.

My grandchildren were encouraged to make things and usually made the gifts which they gave to each other and their parents. While they are making them, they really get excited, often turning out imaginative, beautiful, and thoughtful presents. One year my six-year-old granddaughter suggested that we should all do our Christmas shopping in the house. It was her way of saying we already had a lot of things, much of which we did not use regularly. We followed her advice and shopped in the house for books, clothing, maps, and other useful and under-utilized objects.

In order to lead children to do things for themselves, they should be eating well to obtain energy. What we put into our stomachs will nourish our bodies to function at the highest possible level to gain physical and mental energy. When they have this energy, they are able to pick up on the stimulation of stories and conversation, and to make their own presents and entertainment. It is hard to be creative when you are hungry or malnourished, or addicted to sugar, fat or salt. And people who eat much poor food often feel hungry.

When my children were small, I kept things very simple. For instance, I never rushed too much while making an effort to keep them calm and far from frustration. And when the children would feel frustrated and tense, I would make homemade soup for lunch. I would teach them that disappointment should have a perspective. What difference does it make if you don't go to a party you expected to go to? Don't set yourself up for disappointment.

During the holidays children should have a lot of sleep so they can enjoy themselves. Rushing around with too many frenetic social events upsetting their sleep and proper food needs produces more frustration, stress, and dissatisfaction. As parents we have to relax and place fewer demands on ourselves and our children so we have more rewarding holidays. If you want to take something seriously, don't take it *too* seriously. Keep your perspective in balance, I urged my children.

I would encourage the children to bring their friends home and would ask them questions about school and about their families and their opinions about life's matters. It is important to encourage children to converse using full sentences and to bring out their insights without the maddening repetition of numbing phrases such as "you know" or "kinda," "sorta" or "to be perfectly honest." Their observations used to amuse me. My daughter who does this now, told me that recently, one youngster told her mother that she did not like to be asked opinions about serious matters because it took too much energy to answer. I wonder if it's true that children do not like adults to ask their opinion about daily life today? As I said before, most people don't even converse at dinner today, and even those who want to encourage good conversation sometimes write and ask me what we talked about at the table. How do you tell people that you talked about all kinds of subjects, global, national, local, and about major, minor and trivial subjects at the same time and with children from early childhood to adulthood?

Let Us Talk About Recipes

Recipes should be left a little general so that people can branch out and use their imagination, so that they can use their own judgments. What I am saying is that although I wrote my recipes in this book so that people who have not cooked this kind of food nor eaten it have some specific direction, I don't believe in excessive attention to precision in cooking. As I mentioned in the *Preface*, when I cook I use my own judgment, depending on how many are working with me in the kitchen, or how hungry my family is, and a host of other factors in cooking such as how fast you can work, how flexible you are able to be, and whether and what ingredients are at hand. In other words, for me, non-standardized recipes are a virtue. Besides, leaving a recipe general offers an opening for creativity and trying new things.

The first American cookbook was written in 1796 by Amelia Simmons. In the olden days mostly all recipes were general, no definite quantity was specified and proportions were left to the judgment of the cook. Recipes evolved from one cook to another, from one generation to another, each contributing something along the way. The recipes of earlier days were short and not overly specified.

When I was growing up in Lebanon and, even now, recipe books were rarely used. Recipes were passed from one person to another, using observations and predilections, and personal judgments. One forgets how odd it is that people today are so dependent on cook books until visitors from abroad show their surprise that Americans are reading directions while they cook dinner. In the past, people grew up learning how to cook. Schools and books were not necessary.

This observation about the increase in specificity of directions applies to other parts of life as well. Knitting directions today are more specific than when my children were growing up, and so are directions for how to raise a child in every conceivable situation (such as how to act on the child's first day of school or when a relative visits) which has made me say to young mothers, 'put away the book, and be a mother.' You cannot develop your own judgment out of closeness to your children and their environment if you are always looking for and dependent on directions from psychologists and others who are, after all, remote from an intimate knowledge of your household.

You don't just follow the recipe because it is there. I change my recipes every time I cook, making them a little different although they taste almost the same. Take black-eyed peas as an example. Sometimes I cook them with a little rice and a little broth, sometimes not; sometimes I make soup out of them using a little garlic, lemon juice and some parsley on the top. I play with my cooking because cooking is an art, just like bringing up children is also an art. This means you use your common sense, which means you have to think for yourself and judge for yourself.

Who tells us what tastes good and what does not? Julia Child says it took her years to learn how to eat. Some never do learn how to eat. Our babies are given a formula that provides something like two teaspoons of sugar a feeding and more sugar in baby food. Then we raise them on sweetened frankfurter and hamburger buns, sweet ketchup, candy and drinks. And, Campbell Soup tells us tasty soup contains MSG (monosodium glutamate). Old-fashioned soup is not tasty to youngsters and adults whose taste buds were reared on MSG soup. I'll take old-fashioned home made soup for flavor and nutrients anytime because I was fortunate enough not to have grown up on MSG soup. The quality of the ingredients is important. The stock pot has not disappeared from our family kitchens.

Some of the recipes in this book are entirely my own concoctions, that is, they are not traditional recipes. Every time I cooked lunch or dinner I would say, this dish is for your blood pressure, or this will help your complexion, or this will improve your eyesight. I think that my family has noticed this tendency in me and now they can read about such food/body connections in *The Food Pharmacy* by Jean Carper.

I throw ingredients together, and the result is a bouquet, very good and tasty, food for all the senses, not just a flavor, but also of texture, aroma and sight. I don't think anyone uses many recipes in order to cook a good meal, but people who follow recipes exactly are afraid to venture out. I agree with another Mrs. Child, who in her classic 1832 book, *The American Frugal Housewife*, emphasized the value of living within our means and who also observed that "Wisdom must be gained by a few mistakes." Florence Fabricant recently wrote in *The New York Times*, about her inventive approach to cooking, "This style of cooking takes fundamental skills, some imagination and confidence... Being involved, not merely following formulas is one of cooking's greatest pleasures."

Ways of Living

I clean my house on my hands and knees. I work in the yard and because of these exertions I don't need to pay for exercise classes. Whenever possible, I go barefoot for it makes me feel relaxed and comfortable.

We humans are composed of cells and we should nourish those cells. We are after all what we eat, and the connection between mind and body is often obvious, if we are observant. For instance you should not eat gassy food if you are tense. Plain toast will help to settle your stomach and help you to relax. Life without health is not a good life, and we should go back to mother nature and listen to our bodies. Eat simply and exercise naturally. By that I mean doing something useful which at the same time exercises the body.

When the child gets sick and needs some homemade broth, she will eat it with appreciation because it will make the child feel good. Children have to be trained to eat good food from infancy up, and won't be cranky about it in part because they know it is nutritious or good for them. The loss of natural flavors often means the loss of nutrition. So replacing natural flavors by food processing and additives masks the loss of nutrition. It's not just taste buds that are important. You have to explain how good food contributes to the body's health. And, you have to discipline children to obey. Otherwise, nowadays, they will obey the flood of advertisements and absorb the commercialism that is everywhere. Once, while watching the incessant and loud ads for over-the-counter medicines on the evening television news, I remarked to my grandchildren, that the ads themselves were a headache, with no relief in sight.

I gave the children raw chick peas for snacks. How? Soak them overnight. The next morning wash them well and give them chick peas, instead of chocolate. If you doubt that children will take to this idea, consider that children in many other countries eat snacks such as chick peas and other raw vegetables, fruit and nuts. Sugared prepackaged snacks are a relatively recent business phenomenon. Why can't we build our own sensible community food culture?

I believe that children should have some time to themselves, some solitude. I wanted them to be comfortable being alone with themselves. This is what I intended when I told my daughter Claire she could not sing in the choir, with a group, until she first learned to sing alone. I wanted the children to be able to exercise their minds and understand the importance of solitude, to be self-reliant, to think independently. The children were encouraged to be themselves, to know how to define themselves.

You Should Care

People all over this country make a difference when they contribute to their community. To get interested in the community is the best mental exercise, and provides good educational experiences as well. "You should care" was a conviction in our family. If it is right to do something, do it even if it is a small thing, I always told the children.

When my oldest child, Shafeek, successfully prevented the telephone company from removing a beautiful tree near our home, he learned an important lesson in what civic initiative meant. There were further lessons in civic life when he accompanied his father to the town meetings where Mr. Nader was inquiring about how tax money was being spent and for what purposes. And, another lesson came when Mr. Nader sent his own money and that of other Lebanese immigrants to build a sewer in his home village in Lebanon, only to follow up that project by helping to persuade the town officials of Winsted that they too should get a sewer system laid. Until such proddings, the Mad River, which runs through town, served as the sewage receptacle.

When Ralph was at Princeton University, he saw dead birds in the springtime under trees that had been sprayed with DDT. He protested in a letter to the *Daily Princetonian*. Could this environmental assault not be prevented? His sensitivity and curiousity grew even though his pleas were not accepted at that time.

When the old Gilbert School in Winsted became available for another use because a new Gilbert School had been built, Shafeek thought the wonderful brick building on the Green in the east end of town would make a good home for a two-year community college for the Northwestern region of Connecticut. People were skeptical, even ridiculed the idea that anyone could put a two-year college in such a small town. Nevertheless, against all odds, and together with a few other citizens, Shafeek founded this community college in the fall of 1965.

After the floods of 1955, we needed a dry dam in Winsted. I asked an acquaintance of Senator Prescott Bush to ask the Senator, who was the father of President George Bush, to provide Winsted with a dry dam. She did and his response was a smile only. One day this friend invited Senator Bush to speak, and Mr. Nader and I went to hear him. After the speech I went over to the Senator, introduced myself, and shook hands with him saying, 'Senator Bush, Winsted needs your support in getting the Army Corps of Engineers to build a dry dam.' He smiled and didn't say anything. I wouldn't let go of his hand until he promised to help. And, as matters turned out, with his help and no doubt that of other people also, the Army Corps of Engineers did build the dry dam we needed. We all should remember one reality about our elected representatives. If you want them to go out on a limb for you, make sure to give them a firm trunk.

One time when the librarians at the Beardsley and Memorial Library in Winsted were complaining that the young were not returning the books they had checked out, McDonald's responded with an announcement that they would reward the children who returned their books with a McDonald's hamburger. I thought that was wrong. The children should be taught that the privilege of borrowing books from a free and public library carried with it the responsibility of returning books in good order. We did not let McDonald's bribe our children in Winsted. If the citizen sleeps, everyone sleeps.

The Mary P. Hinsdale elementary school that our children had attended was in need of repair and expansion. The official plan recommended demolition of the big red brick school building, the original structure, and a second addition of space in nondescript motel architectural style. My daughter Claire, joined by other concerned citizens, retained an architect who knew how to blend new and old, and who knew how to build efficiently in a New England environment. The efforts of many citizens concerned with challenging the demolition mentality so often adopted these days when public officials surrender their independent judgment to consulting firms, were heroic. But, unfortunately, in the end we lost "Big Red." However, we won a court decision for the right to vote again on the issue, although too late to stop the steamroller toward a mediocre solution. A full-time, citizen supported community advocate as we now have in Winsted would have helped to alert citizens earlier and to defend their rights in a more organized and timely way.

Quality of food issues are challenging. We would like to be healthy and live long lives. Much of our so-called food in the grocery stores today could probably be avoided and I am sure everybody would be better off and healthier. We know that excessive fat, sugar, and salt detract from our health. I watch how some people shop in grocery stores. It is really a pity to see their carriages so full of junk food.

One day I was watching a young mother with a child filling her basket with junk food. She complained about the prices, and I could not help but say to her that most of the food in her basket was not good for her family. She became interested in what I was saying and wanted to learn how to buy safely and thriftily. So I began showing her what she should buy in nutritious food for far less than the price of her junk food basket. I have begun showing people how to buy without hurting anybody's feelings and have also gotten much satisfaction from doing this.

Recently, I have been interested in the problems facing our local hospital, a community hospital that became enmeshed in what some people call merger mania. We formed a "Watchdog Committee" and invited people to give their views about how we can keep our community hospital in the community. My mother did the same in Lebanon many years ago.

As we grow older, we must stay interested and interesting both in our private and citizen lives, so that we are able to preach what we practice, not only try to practice what we preach. If we love our country and community, we need to work to make them more lovable.

PART TWO

THE FOOD

HELPFUL HINTS FOR THE RECIPES

~ ABOUT EQUIPMENT

My kitchen is a very simple one. It has only the most basic equipment found in many kitchens; for example, pots and pans of various sizes, glass baking dishes, sharp cutlery, a colander, a blender which can be used to grind spices, and a mortar and pestle to pound garlic, herbs and spices. I have an old hand grinder with different parts for fine and coarse grinding of meat, vegetables and nuts, and an electric grinder which also has fine and coarse blades. The food processors tend to pulverize meat or bruise the pieces, but produce a very smooth result for the hummus dish, for example.

What can I tell you that you might need, in addition to such common kitchen tools, to prepare some of the recipes in this book? A corer is essential to core squash and potatoes in preparation for inserting a filling. Also a pastry crimper or tweezers which have a one-fourth inch width to them to use for decorating the nut-filled pastries called ma'mool. For kneading bread I have a commercial dough mixer. I have often kneaded by hand as well.

~ ABOUT FREEZING

TOMATOES. I used to can tomatoes the old fashioned way in jars. Now I freeze them at the height of their season for the winter months, using organically grown tomatoes from a nearby farmer. I cut the tomatoes in wedge-shaped or chunky pieces and freeze in a medium size ziplock bag.

LAMB BROTH. When I make the lamb broth from the lamb bones, which the butcher saves for me, I put the broth in an ice tray to form cubes, or in a refrigerator bag. As you can notice, lamb broth is a mainstay in my recipes.

LAMB MEAT. Meat from the leg of lamb is also a mainstay, and I prepare it ahead of time after the butcher bones the leg of lamb for me. I freeze the meat wrapped in aluminum foil in amounts I usually use in the different recipes. Preparation means removing all fat possible and dividing the meat in two parts, one for kibbi and other recipes requiring the leanest meat and one part for cooking stews and the like where it was not easy to remove the fat. Butchers can do this work for you. However, they do not have the time to be as meticulous as the cook, so I prepare my own.

Once the lamb meat is prepared and frozen, it is quicker to cook the different dishes. Times given for recipes assume readiness of the lamb meat required. Preparing the meat is often an occasion for socializing with family members who help. When such help is available, I order two legs of lamb at one time. There are many such opportunities for family gatherings around cooking.

FREEZING FOOD FOR FUTURE USE. A number of dishes can be partially or fully frozen ahead of time, a boon to busy people, for example, cooked chick peas minus the dressing, rolled grape leaves minus the lemon juice; kibbi, fatayer, and spheeha, cooked or uncooked. Each person can make that decision as familiarity with the various recipes grows.

~ ABOUT INGREDIENTS

MINT. I like to dry my own fresh mint in the sun and then crush well before storing in tightly closed jars. My neighbor has a big plot of mint in his garden and he has dried mint for me, which I always appreciate. (I wish he had a grape arbor so I could have fresh grape leaves.) The ingredient "fresh dried mint" in the recipes refers to mint prepared in this way. Of course, dried mint can also be bought in the grocery stores.

OLIVE OIL. A light variety from the first press is preferable so the oil taste does not overwhelm the food or compete with it.

Some ingredients may be unfamiliar and a note on these may be helpful. You can purchase these ingredients from Middle Eastern or Greek grocery stores or specialty food shops.

MAHLAB is the kernel of a cherry. Ground into a powder it gives a distinctive flavor to ka'ak, the popular sweet yeast bread, and other pastries and breads.

ANISE SEEDS come from a fruit plant. Known also as *Yansoon*, it makes an excellent infusion.

CARDAMOM, a spice from the ginger family, ground or its seed pods crushed slightly, is used in food, including fruit desserts and beverages, especially coffee.

ORANGE FLOWER WATER (MAZAHER) *AND ROSE WATER* (MAWARD) lend a marvelous fragrance and are used in desserts. Their essences are distilled from the petals of the flowers with water.

SESAME SEEDS. An herb plant. A quality oil is extracted from the seeds. They can also be lightly toasted and used in breads and pastries, adding a nutty flavor. *Tahini* used in hummus, baba ghanoogh and other recipes is a paste made from crushed sesame seeds.

SAFFRON, a spice made from the crocus flower, is used with rice, which shows off its familiar yellow color, and other recipes.

ZA'TAR means thyme and refers also to a popular mixture which usually includes two parts thyme, one part sumac (ground from a berry), one part sesame seeds. Za'tar is mixed with olive oil and eaten with Arabic bread.

CORIANDER, an herb in seed or ground form. The plant's green leaves are known as cilantro.

BURGHUL (also known as bulgar, cracked wheat or wheat grain) is available in a fine (#1) and coarse grind (#2 and 3). These descriptors are used interchangeably.

LABAN means yogurt, plain.

KISHK, a powdered cereal made from burghul and laban, is used in a number of dishes.

~ OTHER TIPS

Lemons are wonderful to use in so many ways. In order to get the most juice from each lemon, I soak lemons in hot water to produce more juice.

Just as my kitchen is sparsely equipped, serving the food is equally simple. Many of the recipes are presented on platters and decorated, giving a great opportunity to demonstrate the artistic expression of the cook in welcoming guests. Platters have an aura of hospitality about them because they are spacious and welcoming to any number of unexpected guests. I place a great value on easily expandable recipes, abundant servings and varied dishes at one meal.

Grains and vegetables garnished with meat, provide a little meat flavor without being overwhelming and too much to digest. Fresh fruits, dates and nuts are important foods for our table.

On the time it takes to cook a dish. Some recipes can be made quickly. Within a half hour an entire hearty meal can be on the table. However, there are some that one cannot rush through. Here the approach to cooking comes into play. Think of what else can be gotten out of the meal besides the food on the table. As with the preparation of the leg of lamb, it takes time to core squash or to decorate the ma'mool pastry before baking. Performing these tasks can become a social event. When family or friends are present, they can help in such tasks. And it is so pleasant to have them because I catch up with their lives. Time, then, is not a drawback if one combines social with cooking time.

For a few of the recipes, the preparation/cooking time is variable enough that I have left this determination to the cook.

Regarding the names of recipes, you will notice that I sometimes began with the English description followed by the Arabic name, and sometimes I reversed the order to familiarize the cook right off with the original name. Tabouli is, of course, already well-known as is Hummus and Baba Ghanoogh. A few have no descriptors but the recipe itself.

APPETIZERS

HUMMUS BI TAHINI (Chick Peas with Sesame Seed Paste)

An appetizer which can serve as a light lunch or supper. It attracts the palate and the eye and teases the taste buds. To enhance its subtle flavor, serve at room temperature or cold but not too cold. The hummus, cooked and blended smoothly, can be frozen and kept for future use. The dressing is added at the time of serving. As with baba ghanoogh, hummus bi tahini can be eaten with Arabic bread.

½ pound dried chick peas
   or about 1 cup
1 teaspoon salt
2-3 lemons
2 tablespoons cold water
4-5 sprigs parsley

6 cups cold water
4 garlic cloves
5 generous tablespoons Tahini
1 teaspoon cumin to taste (optional)
2 tablespoons olive oil

PREPARE THE HUMMUS

~ Soak the chick peas overnight in cold water after checking for small stones and blemished chick peas.

~ The next day wash the chick peas well, rinsing them several times.

~ Put chick peas in pot with 6 cups cold water and cook on high heat. Tilt the cover of the pot so there is a way the steam will escape, keeping the foam under control. The chick peas are cooked when a pea can be mashed easily between two fingers.

COMBINE THE HUMMUS WITH THE TAHINI DRESSING

~ Put garlic, lemon juice, chick peas and tahini in blender or food processor, blend until smooth. Follow this procedure three or four times until all the ingredients have been finely blended. If more liquid is needed, add 2 tablespoons cold water, or more lemon juice which will give the hummus a tangy taste.

~ Alternatively, the dressing can be made separately and then combined with hummus. Pound garlic cloves with salt, add the tahini and mix well. Add the lemon juice and mix well. Add cold water or more lemon juice to obtain a more liquid consistency. Mix hummus with the tahini dressing.

~ Serve in a platter cold or at room temperature. Make a design with a fork as grooved highways, putting olive oil across the top. If you wish, you can sprinkle paprika over the hummus for color. Garnish with sprigs of parsley.

TIME: 1 hour.   SERVES : 6.

BABA GHANOOGH (Eggplant with Sesame Seed Paste)

This appetizer can be a light meal in itself. It satisfies the palate and the eye. To keep the subtle flavor of the baba ghanoogh, serve lukewarm or cold but not too cold. After the eggplant is cooked and taken from its skin, you can freeze it for future use, having added the lemon juice to keep it from darkening. I prefer serving this recipe fresh.

2 medium eggplant	3 lemons (or to taste)
3 tablespoons Tahini	3 garlic cloves (or to taste)
½ teaspoon salt	6-8 radishes
3-4 sprigs parsley	Dash of paprika (optional)

~ Wash eggplant, score with knife straight through to allow steam to escape when baking.

~ Bake in shallow pan in 400° F oven until skin can be peeled off easily, about 40 minutes. Cool.

~ Remove eggplant from skin, mash eggplant well in a bowl by hand or in a food processor which produces a smoother consistency.

PREPARE DRESSING

~ Peel and pound garlic well with salt. Add tahini and mix.

~ Add lemon juice and mix well. Additional lemon juice gives a tart taste to the baba ghanoogh. Pour dressing onto eggplant and mix well.

~ Serve in platter and decorate with radishes (fashioned into florets or cut into segments or minced) and sprigs of parsley at two ends of the platter. You can also sprinkle paprika on the top for color.

TIME: 1 hour.   SERVES: 6.

SALMON

This appetizer begins a meal with an elegant touch.

2 pounds salmon, fresh fillet
2 lemons
1 tablespoon olive oil or butter
½ teaspoon tarragon or curry powder (or to taste)
4 slices whole wheat bread

~ Broil salmon with lemon juice and olive oil or butter, and tarragon or curry powder.

~ Toast the bread and cut each piece in half.

~ Serve salmon in small dish with toasted bread.

TIME: 20 minutes.   SERVES: 8.

CHICKEN SPREAD

This spread is convenient and substantial. It can also be made with turkey.

3½ pounds chicken
2 medium onions
3 celery stalks with leaves
½ bunch parsley
½ teaspoon poultry seasoning
½ teaspoon thyme
1 cinnamon stick

~ Boil chicken in cold water, barely covering, for a few minutes. Throw water out and rinse the fowl, removing skin.

~ Return fowl to pot, cover with cold water, adding cinnamon stick, salt and pepper, and cook until done.

~ Grind the meat finely with celery stalks including the leaves, parsley with stems, and onions.

~ Season with salt, poultry seasoning and thyme.

~ Serve spread on a cracker or whole wheat or other dark bread.

~ Or: Form into round flat shapes, place in pan greased with butter, and bake in 350° F oven until slightly brown.

TIME: 1 hour 10 minutes.   SERVES: 20 - 25.

SOUPS

LAMB BROTH

This broth is a staple in many of my recipes. Freeze it in cubes or refrigerator bags and use as wanted for making soup, rice or as called for in these recipes.

Bones from leg of lamb
Cold water

~ Boil lamb bones briefly in water to cover, using 4 quart pot. Then discard water and rinse bones.

~ Boil bones 4-5 hours in pot, covering bones with cold water, almost to the top. Use low heat and boil until the liquid reduces about one half. The meat on the bones should easily fall off the bones.

~ Strain the broth and refrigerate over night. The next morning skim off the fat and discard.

~ The meat can be taken off the bones and used in cooking a light lunch, for example, mixing an egg in for an omelet.

TIME: 5 hours.

LAMB BROTH SOUP

This soup leaves you with a wonderful feeling of the hearth. Excellent when not feeling well, light and nourishing.

3 cups lamb broth
1 cup burghul or barley or long grain brown rice
1 stalk celery
2 medium onions or scallions
4-5 garlic cloves
4 carrots
1 green pepper
1 bunch parsley

~ Cut into small pieces celery, onions, carrots (first scraped) and green pepper.

~ Put lamb broth in pot and heat on low heat if frozen. Add the above ingredients and the burghul or barley or rice. Then cook on low heat, seasoning with salt and pepper to taste. Add water if needed.

~ Before serving, add minced parsley.

TIME: ½ hour   SERVES: 4.

BLACKEYED PEA SOUP

Simple food that will warm you from the tips of your toes to the roots of your hairs and fill all the empty places in between. Delicious with whole wheat bread and salad.

1 pound blackeyed peas
2 cups cold water
4 cups lamb broth
5-7 garlic cloves
2 tablespoons fresh dried mint

~ Wash beans and add cold water and broth. Season with salt and pepper to taste. Cook until well done. Add water, if needed.

~ After peas are cooked, put garlic, mint and some of the beans in blender on chop and then on puree. Blend the rest of the peas.

~ Heat on low heat and serve.

TIME: 45 minutes.   SERVES: 6.

LENTIL-SOYBEAN SOUP

Another simple, fully satisfying dish.

1 cup lentils
½ cup olive oil
4 garlic cloves
3 carrots
½ cup fresh parsley
Salt, pepper and cinnamon
   to taste

1 cup soy beans
3 medium onions
5 cups cold water
6 stalks of celery tops
1 lemon

~ Soak soybeans overnight with cold water. Save the water for cooking. Wash lentils.

~ Cook soybeans and lentils using 5 cups of water, adding sliced onions, garlic and olive oil, until half done.

~ Then add the rest of the ingredients which you have cut into small pieces. Season to taste and cook until done. Use a low fire to get a savory taste. Cover the ingredients well with water and when you think more is needed, add more, but use cold not hot water.

~ Chop and add the parsley a few minutes before serving.

TIME: 1½ hours.   SERVES: 6.

CUCUMBERS WITH LABAN

This dish is wonderfully tasty as appetizer, side dish, or as a cool summer soup for lunch or supper.

2 cucumbers
2½ cups laban
5-6 garlic cloves (if you like garlic, less otherwise)
1 tablespoon fresh dried mint
Several dashes of salt

~ Pound garlic with salt and dried mint.

~ Peel and cut cucumbers into slices

~ Add laban to cucumbers, garlic and dried mint mixture.

~ Stir well and serve cold.

TIME: 10 minutes.   SERVES: 4.

SALADS

TABOULI (Parsley, Scallions and Tomatoes with Burghul)

A refreshing, nutritious, colorful salad. Makes an elegant entrée for a summer meal. Refrigerated tabouli stays fresh for several days.

3 bunches parsley

2-3 bunches scallions

4 tablespoons fresh dried mint or 4 sprigs of fresh mint

½ cup olive oil (or to taste)

1 cup fine burghul #1

5 tomatoes

8 lemons (or to taste)

1 head of Romaine lettuce (or more as needed)

~ Cut off stems of parsley with fingers, leaving the florets.

~ Pick leaves off mint stems, if fresh mint is used.

~ Wash parsley in bowl of water, rinsing and draining until all sand has disappeared. Drain well. Wash mint.

~ Mince the parsley very fine, using a knife. If you use a machine chopper, try to leave the parsley perky not mashed. Cut the mint in small pieces.

~ Wash burghul, squeeze the water out by hand and add to above.

~ Add minced scallions, 3 tomatoes minced, and lemon juice until tart taste has been achieved. Add olive oil to taste.

~ Season with salt and pepper.

~ Wash lettuce and separate leaves. Drain well.

~ Serve in a platter. Place a bed of lettuce on platter and put the tabouli over it. Decorate the top with thin slices of 2 tomatoes and small pieces of lettuce all the way around the platter so that these can be used with each serving.

TIME: ½ hour.   SERVES: 10.

FATOOSH (Tomatoes, Scallions and Parsley with Toasted Bread)

A wonderful, colorful summer or winter lunch or supper. Children find fatoosh very satisfying and, as you read on, you will see why.

6 slices whole wheat bread	2 tablespoons cold water
4-5 garlic cloves	2-3 cucumbers
2-3 red and green bell peppers	1 bunch parsley
2 bunches scallions	3-4 tomatoes, the juicy variety
½ head of Romaine lettuce	3-4 lemons
3-4 tablespoons fresh dried mint	½ cup olive oil (or to taste)

~ Toast bread and cut into small pieces.

~ Sprinkle with water to moisten the toast somewhat, and mix.

~ Pound garlic with 1/8 teaspoon salt in a large bowl.

~ Put bread on top of mashed garlic.

~ Cut cucumbers in small chunks, peppers in small pieces, also tomatoes and lettuce; mince parsley with stems and scallions. Put all these vegetables over the bread.

~ Add dried mint, lemon juice, olive oil and salt and pepper to taste.

~ Mix very well with your hands so that all the ingredients are distributed evenly, producing a tasty meal.

TIME: ½ hour.   SERVES: 6 - 8.

POTATO SALAD

This salad is delicious hot or cold! It can even be served as the main dish for a meal.

8-10 small red potatoes
5-6 garlic cloves
1 bunch parsley
1 bunch scallions
1/8 cup olive oil
1-2 lemons (to taste)
1 teaspoon cumin

~ Cook potatoes leaving them firm, not overcooked.

~ Cut potatoes into small chuncks with the skin, if organic.

~ Pound garlic with little salt and add fresh lemon juice.

~ Chop parsley (without stems) and scallions and add to potatoes.

~ Add olive oil, cumin, season with salt and pepper and mix well. Avoid a mushy consistency.

TIME: 35 minutes.   SERVES: 6.

SALATA (Tossed Salad)

This is a hearty salad and when combined with a simple dish makes a fulfilling meal.

2 garlic cloves (more if you like garlic)   Pinch of salt
¼ cup white vinegar or fresh lemon juice   ¼ cup olive oil
2 3 tomatoes   1 cucumber
1 green pepper   1-1½ heads of Romaine
½ bunch watercress   lettuce
Mint (fresh or dried)

~ Pound garlic with salt and add vinegar or fresh lemon juice and olive oil.

~ Add tomatoes cut in small chunks, and cucumber, green pepper and watercress cut into small pieces. Cucumbers may be sliced.

~ Cut or hand tear the lettuce in smallish pieces and add to above.

~ Add dried or fresh mint.

~ Put in refrigerator until time to serve. During this time the lettuce becomes even crisper and the aroma of the dressing seeps through the ingredients, especially if you cover the salad bowl.

~ To serve toss well so that dressing is evenly distributed throughout the salad.

TIME: 15 minutes.   SERVES: 4 - 6.

SWISS CHARD SALAD

A refreshing, nutty, zesty taste, good roughage. To be savored in the eating, particularly if the swiss chard has been grown without the use of pesticides. The leaves tend to be more tender.

1 bunch swiss chard
½ bunch scallions
1/8 cup or less of olive oil
1/8 cup pine nuts

~ Wash swiss chard and cut into small pieces and drain well.

~ Dice scallions and add to the swiss chard.

~ Add pine nuts, olive oil and season to taste.

TIME: 10 minutes.   SERVES: 6.

MAIN DISHES
WITH MEAT

SHAYKH IL MIHSHEE (Baked Eggplant Stuffed with Lamb and Pine Nuts)

This is the shaykh or king of stuffed food, and one of Ralph's favorites. Use the smallest eggplant available. Very small ones are cooked whole, while medium ones (preferably on the small side) are cut in half lengthwise. Served with long grain rice and tossed salad, it is a complete meal.

4 medium eggplant (or ten small)
2 pounds lamb meat (boned leg
  of lamb, fat removed)
8-10 cherry tomatoes (optional)
2 cups lamb broth
2 tablespoons olive oil

2 large or 3 medium onions
2/3 cups pine nuts
4 medium small or 2 very
  large fresh tomatoes
1/8 teaspoon cinnamon (2
  brief shakes from slotted
  top)

PREPARE THE EGGPLANT

~ Wash and trim stem from medium eggplant. Peel, leaving skin on intermittently as in columns. Cut eggplant in half from top to bottom (leave small eggplant whole) and steam over medium heat (in covered saucepan) for 15 - 20 minutes until the skin is soft or the eggplant indents when poked with the finger.

~ Spread small film of olive oil on 9x13x2 inch pan. Place steamed eggplant in pan. If using small eggplant, cut each from top to bottom (boat shape) to permit stuffing to be added. Let eggplant cool to facilitate stuffing.

PREPARE THE STUFFING

~ Grind lamb meat and onions together, using coarse blade. There should be about 2 ¾ cups.

~ Place lamb and onions in saucepan with cinnamon, salt and pepper. Cook over low heat, stirring to avoid sticking. Add pine nuts after 5 minutes. Cook for about 10-12 minutes, until all pink is gone from lamb. Remove from heat.

PREPARE THE ENTIRE DISH

~ While the stuffing is cooking, gently boil fresh tomatoes in uncovered saucepan with two cups of lamb broth until soft and juicy (10-15 minutes).

~ Optional: For decorative effect, cook 8-10 cherry tomatoes in tomato/broth mixture to sit on top of stuffed eggplant.

~ Spoon lamb stuffing on top of split eggplant, pressing the stuffing against the eggplant to secure it. Stuff generously.

~ Place a chunk (several for larger eggplant) of fresh (or canned) tomatoes or the cherry tomatoes on top of each eggplant boat. Spoon remaining tomato broth mixture around the eggplant boats. It should almost cover stuffed eggplant boats.

~ Bake uncovered in oven at 350° F for 30-40 minutes. Add juice as needed.

~ Serve with rice.

TIME: 1½ hours.   SERVES: 6.

SFEEHA OR FATAYER (Open-Faced or Stuffed Pastry with Lamb Filling)

A most filling meal! Sfeeha is open and visibly beckons the pallet. Fatayer is closed and shaped like a three-cornered hat. I usually make these with whole wheat bread dough, although below you will find another version of dough for Sfeeha and Fatayer which uses olive oil.

1 tablespoon or one small cake of yeast

4 cups whole wheat flour (½ white & ½ whole wheat if you wish)

2 pounds lamb meat (boned leg of lamb, fat removed)

2 juicy lemons

¼ cup cold milk

½ cup barely warm milk (use more if needed to make dough)

3 medium or 2 large onions

½ cup pine nuts (use more if desired)

PREPARE THE DOUGH

~ In large bowl, dissolve yeast with cold milk (hot milk prevents bread from rising.)

~ Add flour, and enough barely warm milk to make good, malleable bread dough.

~ Knead well for about 15 minutes by hand or with kneading machine Keep dipping hands in small bowl of milk during kneading process, wiping the side of the bowl with milk-laden hands to clean it as well. The dough should be completely mixed and glistening, and the pan and hands completely clean when kneading is completed. It's great exercise for upper body and arms!

~ Cover bread bowl (with another bowl) and set aside to rise.

~ Pull off small pieces of slightly elastic dough (size of double walnut). Roll them into small balls, place on work surface, and flatten gently with hand.

PREPARE THE FILLING

~ Grind lean lamb meat together with onions, using coarse blade. Season with salt and pepper, add lemon juice and pine nuts.

PREPARE SFEEHA AND FATAYER

~ To make sfeeha, flatten each ball of dough into a circle with fingers, being careful not to flatten edges as much as interior. Place 3 teaspoons of the uncooked filling on each circle with small edge of dough showing. Give filling a gentle push down to secure.

~ To make fatayer, evenly flatten each ball of dough into a circle with fingers, and place 2 teaspoons of filling in center. Make each into the shape of a closed three-cornered hat by pulling dough on opposite sides of circle out and up, and pinching them together on the top and one side. Pull remaining side of dough and pinch each edge against rest of circle to enclose filling completely.

~ Bake in preheated 375° F oven about 20 minutes (until dough is barely browned) on flat cookie sheet greased lightly with olive oil. Sfeeha can be broiled for a minute or two to make crispy.

~ Optional: garnish filling with pomegranates.

TIME: 1 hour to prepare   SERVES: 6.
           20 minutes a tray to bake

DOUGH FOR SFEEHA OR FATAYER

1 or 2 yeast cakes
4 cups flour (whole wheat or
   combination of whole wheat
   and unbleached white flour)

¼ cup cold water
1 cup olive oil
1 tablespoon butter
½ cup milk or more if needed

~ Put the yeast and water in a bowl and dissolve well. Then add the rest of the ingredients and knead very well until your hands look very clean, dipping hands in water if necessary to keep dough from sticking to hands.

SHISHBARAK (Stuffed Bread Dough in Labaneeye or Kishk)

This dish takes patience but the end result is worth the effort.
Shishbarak is especially good on a cold winter day. The directions
for this recipe are as I would give them to my family.

I have not indicated amounts of dough or filling, or labaneeye (p. 72) needed because amounts depend on the number of persons to be served. Whatever is left over from dough, filling or labaneeye can be used individually the next day. Dough can be made into bread, filling can be used for lunch adding an egg to it and labaneeye is good hot soup by itself. So don't be timid about making this recipe.

Page references of recipes required for Shishbarak are indicated in the directions.

Roll bread dough thin (p. 144). Cut pieces 2 inches in diameter using, for example, a wine glass. Fill with same filling used for Shaykh il Mihshee (p. 62). Close and shape like a crescent. Bring the two ends together and press tightly. Bake the crescents on a greased tray until dough is slightly browned. Put the crescents in the pot with the labaneeye but omit the rice. Cook slowly for about 10 minutes.

Time: Keep track of how long it took you and complete for your reference.

Serves (add your own number).

KIBBI (Ground Lamb with Wheat Grain)

Kibbi is the national dish of Lebanon and there are many ways to prepare and serve Kibbi. It is a favorite dish because of its delicate flavors and the variety of methods for preparation of the finished dish. It can be baked with a filling of lamb with pine nuts and cinnamon, it can be made into meat patties, it can be shaped into an egg, filled and cooked in labaneeye, it can be shaped into balls and cooked in hot broth and tomato sauce, and more. Enjoy the journey.

3 pounds lamb meat (boned leg of lamb, fat removed)
3 medium onions
2 cups fine burghul #1

PREPARE BASIC KIBBI

1. Grind meat and onions together using fine blade.

2. Wash burghul and then squeeze water well from grain by hand.

3. Mix burghul with meat and onion well, preferably by hand.

4. Season with salt and pepper.

5. Grind total mixture a second time.

6. Mix with hands, using a little water to make the mixture pliable and smooth.

TIME: 15 minutes.   SERVES: 8 - 10

FILLING FOR KIBBI (if called for)

½ pound lamb meat (boned leg of lamb, fat removed)
½ teaspoon cinnamon

1 medium onion
2/3 cup pine nuts
1 teaspoon lemon juice

PREPARE FILLING

1. Grind meat and onion together using fine blade.

2. Cook for several minutes, seasoning with salt, pepper and cinnamon.

3. Add pine nuts and cook for another 10 minutes until the lamb is no longer pink.

TIME: 20 minutes.

SIX WAYS OF PREPARING KIBBI DISHES

BAKED KIBBI

1/3 pound butter

1. Butter a 2 inch high 9x12 pan, glass or stainless steel, with a small amount of the butter, (reserve ¼ pound for top of dish).

2. Spread basic uncooked Kibbi mixture about ½ inch thick, smoothing and gently pressing it down by hand, using a little water sprinkled from the hand. It should be very smooth.

3. Spread a thin layer of cooked filling. Pat the surface and gently smooth it by hand.

4. Spread a second layer of uncooked Kibbi mixture about 1/3 inch thick. Once again pat the surface, using water sprinkled by hand to make it very smooth.

5. With a wet, sharp knife, gently cut the kibbi with evenly spaced diagonal lines across the longer end of the pan and then along the shorter end, to create diamond shaped pieces. Cut with an up and down motion, as in cutting a cake, to avoid disturbing the smooth surface and the filling.

6. With wet knife, gently loosen the Kibbi from the edges of the pan, and then score the center of each diamond shaped piece by just inserting the knife and removing it. This will allow butter to penetrate the center of each piece.

7. Make a hole about the size of a nickle in the center of the Kibbi mixture with the middle finger.

8. Spread the ¼ pound butter across the top of the pan, placing some in the hole.

9. Bake in the bottom shelf of a 350° F oven for 45-60 minutes, depending on oven. You will know it is done if the Kibbi moves when you wiggle the pan.

10. Remove from oven, sprinkle with cold water thrown from the hand once. Cover with a tray, cookie sheet or pan until it is served (Kibbi can be eaten cold, but many prefer it warm right out of the oven).

TIME: 1 hour 20 minutes.   SERVES: 8 - 10.

KIBBI PATTIES BROILED (Kibbi Mishweeye)

1. Form basic uncooked Kibbi mixture into patties about 3-4 inches in diameter.

2. Baste top of each patty with olive oil (optional). Grease tray with olive oil.

3. Broil in 350° F oven until brown on top. Then turn over until brown again. Do not overcook, as the Kibbi will dry out.

SERVES: 8 - 10.

STUFFED KIBBI

1. Place a small amount of raw basic Kibbi mixture in the palm of the hand. Form it into an oval shape.

2. While cupping and rotating the Kibbi with one hand, core into the middle of the oval from the long end with the forefinger of the other hand, making a hollow space to permit insertion of the filling. The sides of the Kibbi should be as thin as feasible. It should resemble a hollow egg.

3. Put about 1 teaspoon of cooked Kibbi filling into the hollowed egg shaped form. Gently close the opening or mouth, using a splash of water to smooth it closed.

4. Broil on tray greased with olive oil in 350° F oven until a little brown; then turn the Kibbis and broil the underside until brown. Do not overcook, as Kibbi will dry out.

SERVES: 8 - 10.

STUFFED KIBBI COOKED IN LABANEEYE *

5-6 garlic cloves
¼ teaspoon butter
1 quart cold water
1 egg

1 teaspoon salt
2 quarts laban (p. 147)
¼ cup uncooked long grain brown rice
Mint (preferably fresh but dried is ok) use generously to taste

1. Pound garlic with salt and plenty of chopped fresh or dried mint.

2. Place laban, cold water, rice and egg in large 5 quart cooking pot. The egg is important to prevent the laban from separating when it is heated. Season with salt.

3. With a manual egg beater (or electric one on low), beat this mixture in the pot until the labaneeye begins to boil and bubbles are evident.

4. When labaneeye is boiling, add 5 or 6 stuffed Kibbi (be sure they are completely closed and sealed) and cook for a few minutes. The stuffed Kibbi is cooked when it bounces back after being gently tapped with a spoon. It will sound hollow.

Note: If the stuffed Kibbi sinks when tapped, this means it was not completely closed and liquid has seeped inside. If this happens, simply finish cooking. It's not a disaster.

5. Cook the remaining stuffed Kibbi, 5 or 6 at one time. Place the stuffed cooked Kibbi on platter and cover to keep warm.

6. Place Kibbi and labaneeye mixture in a large bowl or soup tureen. Serve Kibbi with labaneeye spooned over it in soup bowls.

SERVES: 8 - 10

* Kishk may be used in place of labaneeye. It is considered a delicacy and a very welcome food gift. Wonderful for a cold, bleak wintery day. Fuels the body and warms the soul!

KIBBI IN TOMATO SAUCE

1. Form Kibbi into elongated solid balls and bake until slightly brown. Set aside and make the sauce.

PREPARE THE SAUCE

5 onions
5-6 fresh tomatoes or fresh frozen
3 cups broth

6-7 garlic cloves
3 tablespoons olive oil
½ cup cold water

2. Slice onions and garlic and cut tomatoes in chunks if fresh. If frozen, they are already cut in chunks.

3. Place broth and water in pot and season with salt and pepper. Add above mixture and cook on low heat.

4. Add the kibbi and stir gently.

5. Serve on rice.

SERVES: 8 - 10.

KIBBI WITH KISHK AND VEGETABLES

1 lamb shank and several lamb bones
½ teaspoon cinnamon
2 cups uncooked chick peas, soaked
  overnight in bowl of water
1 teaspoon butter

8 cups water
½ small cabbage, shredded
1 cup kishk
¼ teaspoon coriander
3 large garlic cloves

1. Boil lamb shank (the muscle) and lamb bones in a large pot with water for about 3 hours after seasoning with salt, pepper, and cinnamon.

2. Strain the soup through a colander, returning liquid to the pot. Reserve the lamb parts.

3. Place raw shredded cabbage and uncooked (softened because of the overnight soaking) chick peas in soup and cook for one hour.

4. Remove any lamb meat from bones and shank and place the meat (not the bones) into the hot soup mixture.

5. Cover kishk with 8 cups of cold water, stir to dissolve it, and add it to the hot soup mixture to thicken it.

6. Cut garlic into pieces, then pound garlic with the coriander into the butter and add to the hot thickened soup mixture.

7. Make small balls of raw kibbi and place them in the hot soup mixture. Cook at a slight boil until the kibbi is cooked, about 25 minutes.

8. Serve over hot rice (p. 146).

SERVES: 8 - 10.

CHICKEN WITH LAMB AND RICE (Dajaje ma'a Hashwee)

This chicken dish, dressed up with lamb, nuts and cinnamon, has a familiar and yet delightfully unique taste. It's also a low fat, high energy dish.

3½ pounds chicken
2 pounds lean lamb meat
  (boned leg of lamb, fat removed)
¼ teaspoon cinnamon
¼ teaspoon poultry seasoning
½ teaspoon cardamom

1 cup long grain rice,
  preferably brown
½ cup pine nuts
½ cup slivered or split
  blanched almonds

PREPARE THE CHICKEN

~ To clean chicken, quickly boil it covered with cold water in 4 or 5 quart pot with two teaspoons of salt. After it comes to a complete boil, throw the water out, rinse the chicken and remove its skin.

~ Cover chicken with cold water, about 3 inches above chicken, to allow 3 cups of broth to remain (for the stuffing) after the chicken is cooked. Season chicken with 1/8 teaspoon cinnamon, poultry seasoning, salt and pepper to taste. Cook covered over high heat to get boiling and then for about 1 hour over moderate heat until chicken pulls easily from bone. Debone and keep chicken pieces ample.

PREPARE THE STUFFING

~ Grind lamb meat using coarse blade. Wash and drain rice. Place lamb, rice, pine nuts, almonds, 1/8 teaspoon cinnamon, and salt and pepper to taste, in saucepan with 2-3 cups of chicken broth.

~ Cook slowly with pot covered about 30 minutes or until rice is separate and not sticking together.

PREPARE TO SERVE

~ Mix the stuffing and the chicken pieces and serve on large platter. Reserve several good-sized chicken pieces and place on top of entire dish.

TIME: 1 hour 50 minutes.   SERVES: 6 - 8.

CHICKEN IN CASSEROLE

This dish is a new experience in chicken. A succulent combination of chicken and vegetables steamed into one another.

One whole chicken, about 3½ pounds
½ teaspoon cinnamon
1 bunch carrots (or more if desired)
2 pound package frozen peas (or 1 pound fresh peas shelled)

1 cup rice
½ teaspoon poultry seasoning
1 bunch celery
1 large bunch parsley
4 bunches green scallions

~ Clean and wash chicken and remove all skin, if easy, otherwise after boiling. Put into 3 or 4 quart pot and cover with cold water. Bring to boil, and then throw the water out, rinse the chicken and return to the pot. Cover again with cold water.

~ Season chicken with salt, pepper, cinnamon and poultry seasoning. Cook over medium heat until chicken meat is so tender it pulls away easily from the bone. Remove chicken from pot to a large platter

~ While chicken is cooking, wash and cut celery and carrots into small pieces. After chicken is removed from broth, add carrots and celery pieces and cook in broth until half done. Shell peas (if fresh are used) and add to other vegetables, cooking until almost done.

~ In the meantime, wash rice well (use colander or strainer). Add rice to vegetables and chicken broth and cook until almost done. Broth will mostly be gone by this time.

~ While vegetables and rice are cooking, separate chicken from bone into mouth size pieces, mince the parsley, and cut scallions into small pieces. Mix rice, vegetables, adding frozen peas (if used instead of fresh peas), with chicken, parsley and scallions in a 3 or 4 quart casserole.

~ Bake casserole in preheated oven at 350° F for 20-25 minutes.

TIME: 1½ hours.   SERVES: 8 - 10.

ROAST TURKEY

Making roast turkey is special because each family member knows whether it tastes 'right' or not. This is my traditional roast turkey recipe that the children still look for.

1 16 pound turkey	½ fresh lemon
½ teaspoon cinnamon	2 tablespoons olive oil
1 loaf of whole wheat bread	2 cups hot milk
1 bunch celery	5-6 medium onions
3 tablespoons butter	1 bunch parsley, minced
1 teaspoon thyme	1 teaspoon poultry seasoning

PREPARE THE TURKEY

~ Wash the turkey thoroughly inside and out. Rub lemon inside and out. Season by rubbing with salt, pepper, cinnamon inside and out. Grease outside with olive oil.

PREPARE BREAD STUFFING

~ To prepare the stuffing, cube toasted whole wheat bread. Add milk and mix well. Chop celery and onion into tiny pieces, saute in butter, and add to the bread mixture. Add thyme and poultry seasoning, salt and pepper. Add minced parsley just before stuffing the turkey.

~ Stuff turkey with bread stuffing.

~ Roast the stuffed turkey on a rack very slowly in a 250° F oven. You can tell if the turkey is done with a meat thermometer, or by pinching the legs and skin. If they move, it is done.

TIME: About 20 minutes per pound, depending on your oven.   SERVES: 12 - 14.

LAMB STEW WITH LIMA OR STRING BEANS (Yakhnat Loubieh)

This country stew is self-contained and leaves one fully satisfied while light on calories.

2 pounds lamb meat (boned leg of lamb, fat removed)
3 medium onions
4 packages of frozen lima beans
        or
3½ pounds fresh string beans
3 fresh tomatoes
1½ cups cold water

~ Cut lamb meat into 2 inch chunks.

~ Brown lamb meat slightly in large 3 quart pot, seasoning with salt and pepper.

~ Add sliced onions and cook stirring frequently, until meat is somewhat tender.

~ Add string beans or lima beans, whichever one is selected. Add tomatoes cut In chunks.

~ Add cold water so stew is juicy. Cover and cook over medium low heat for 10-15 minutes. Stir and then continue to cook until the beans are done, about 45 minutes.

~ Serve with rice.

TIME: 1 hour 15 minutes.   SERVES: 8.

BAKED OKRA WITH LAMB (Bamieh ma'a Lahm)

If you don't try this recipe because you don't usually like okra, you may not know what you're missing. Pure succulence.

5 boxes frozen okra or 3½ pounds fresh
2½ pounds lamb meat (boned leg of
   lamb, fat removed)
1 tablespoon coriander (or more
   for taste
2 lemons

1½ tablespoons butter
2 large onions
8 garlic cloves
3½ tablespoons fresh dried
   mint
1 cup lamb broth (p. 50)

~ Brown frozen okra in 3 quart baking dish in oven with butter. If fresh okra is used, wash it well, soak overnight in red cooking wine to cover. The next day drain okra and brown in oven as with frozen okra. Discard wine.

~ Cut lamb meat into chunks and saute over medium heat with a tablespoon of water to avoid sticking until they are slightly browned, about 15 minutes.

~ Add sliced onions and cook until onions are transparent and slightly browned.

~ Pound coriander with dried mint and garlic together (or mix them in a blender). Add this mixture to the lamb and onions.

~ Add lamb broth. Pour lamb mixture over okra into baking dish. Bake for one hour at 350° F (or less as needed).

~ Serve with rice (p. 146).

TIME: 1 hour 15 minutes.   SERVES: 7 - 8.

EGGPLANT STEW (Yakhnat Beitinjan)

This is a simple and wholesome main course. It tastes wonderful the second day as well.

1 pound lamb (boned leg of lamb, fat removed)
5 medium onions
5 large garlic cloves
3 medium size eggplants
3 medium zucchini
4 medium boiling potatoes
5 fresh tomatoes (or 1 ziplock bag of 5 fresh frozen tomatoes cut in
  chunks or 1 28 oz. can)
Herbs of choice

~ Cube lamb, season with salt and pepper and sauto for a fow minutes over low heat in 5 quart pot. Add sliced onions and garlic, sauté over medium heat until meat has a touch of brown.

~ Cube raw eggplant, removing skin, but leaving a little for appearance. Cube raw zucchini and potatoes, removing skin unless organic and then as desired. Cut tomatoes in chunks.

~ Add remaining ingredients to browned lamb, with herbs if you want, cover and cook about 30 minutes over medium heat. This dish can also be cooked in the oven. Serve with rice.

TIME: 55 minutes.   SERVES: 6 - 8.

LAMB PATTIES WITH SPINACH (Kaftas ma'a Yakhnat Sabaneeckh)

This dish provides unique tastes and texture, but is not difficult to prepare. If you like spinach, you'll love this recipe.

2½ pounds lamb (boned leg of lamb, fat removed

5 slices whole wheat bread

¼ cup pine nuts

3 large garlic cloves

1 tablespoon olive oil

5 medium onions

½ bunch parsley

2 pounds fresh spinach

1 quart laban (yogurt)

¼ cup fresh dried mint

1 sweet red pepper for garnish

PREPARE LAMB

~ Grind 2 pounds meat with 3 onions, using fine blade. Mix in minced parsley by hand. Form into small kaftas, meat patties 1½-2 inches in diameter.

~ Broil in pan greased lightly with olive oil, for about 12 minutes.

PREPARE SPINACH MIXTURE

~ Mince two onions and ½ pound lamb. Sauté over medium heat with pine nuts, stirring occasionally so it will not stick, for about 10 minutes (half done).

~ Wash spinach well, including stems. Add spinach to lamb and onions, and cook covered for another 10 minutes until spinach is done but not overcooked.

PREPARE LABAN MIXTURE

~ Toast whole wheat bread and cut roughly into about 1 inch pieces. Pound garlic. Mix toast and garlic with mint and laban.

PREPARE TO SERVE

~ Put half the laban mixture in spacious bowl or deep platter. Add spinach mixture on top. Add remainder of laban mixture. Place broiled kaftas around the side of the bowl or platter. Garnish top with sweet red peppers cut into strips.

TIME: About 1 hour.   SERVES: 8.

ZUCCHINI STUFFED WITH LAMB AND RICE (Koosa Mihshee)

This is a unique presentation of a main dish, containing the taste of meat but a small amount to digest. The trick to preparation is the tool for coring the zucchini and buying short, fat zucchini to make the job easy. The stuffing is the same as for rolled grape leaves and rolled cabbage. It can be prepared ahead of time and refrigerated.

1 dozen medium zucchini (short and fat). Yellow summer squash or short green squash can also be used.

4 hefty garlic cloves

3 tablespoons fresh dried mint

1 pint water

2 pounds lamb meat (boned leg of lamb, fat removed)

¾ cup uncooked long grain rice (preferably brown)

1 fresh tomato chopped in small pieces

4 fresh tomatoes cut in chunks

1/8 teaspoon cinnamon (few shakes of slotted container)

PREPARE ZUCCHINI

~ Wash and cut narrow end off of zucchini. Carefully core the zucchini with coring tool, removing and reserving interior pieces. When fully cored, the zucchini should be almost hollow, with fat end in tact. Be careful not to pierce the opposite end or the sides (although it's not a disaster if this happens).

~ Pound garlic with little salt, and mix with dried mint and water. Rinse the cored zucchini in this mixture before stuffing. Save the water for the cooking stage.

PREPARE STUFFING

~ Grind lamb meat, using coarse blade. Mix with rice and chopped tomato. Season with cinnamon, salt and pepper.

~ Using fingers, gently stuff zucchini until about ¾ full. Gently tap bottom of zucchini against work table to get stuffing fully into zucchini, but do not pack tightly or stuff to the brim, as the rice will cook and expand as it absorbs water.

PREPARE FINAL COOKING

~ Cover bottom of large pot (at least 5 quarts), with reserved zucchini pieces. Neatly arrange koosas in pot, layering them on top of each other. Add tomato chunks and reserved pint of mint/garlic water in which zucchini were rinsed. Water will cover some of the zucchini. There should be enough water to steam koosas for one hour. Add water if needed.

~ Place pot over high heat to boil water, then lower heat and cook very slowly for about one hour. Zucchini should be fully cooked and tender (a lighter color of green), but not mushy.

~ Serve hot on platter. Serve with laban.

TIME: 1 hour 45 minutes.:   SERVES: 4 - 6.

ROLLED STUFFED GRAPE LEAVES (Yabrak Arish)

Stuffed with lamb and rice, this delicacy has become popular but is often found doused in heavy olive oil. Steamed and served hot or cold, this recipe contains no added fat products. The grape leaves can be prepared ahead of time, and refrigerated or frozen uncooked, leaving out the lemon juice and water until you cook them.

1 16 ounce jar of grape leaves or fresh grape leaves

¾ cup of long grain uncooked rice, preferably brown

3 tablespoons fresh dried mint

1 cup water

2 pounds lamb meat (boned leg of lamb, fat removed)

1/8 teaspoon cinnamon

3 large garlic cloves

2-3 lemons

~ To prepare fresh grape leaves for rolling, dip them in boiling water for about 30 seconds.

~ Grind lamb meat with coarse blade. Mix with rice, season with salt, pepper and cinnamon.

~ Remove stem from each leaf. Spread each grape leaf on flat work surface. Place about 1 teaspoon of stuffing across the leaf about ½ inch from the stem point. Fold leaf forward toward stuffing, then fold the right side over, then the left, and then roll the leaf forward very tightly. When fully rolled, squeeze it to secure.

~ Repeat this process for each leaf.

~ Put four grape leaves and rough pieces on bottom of 5 quart pot. Neatly place each rolled stuffed grape leaf in the pot in layers.

~ Pound garlic with mint and salt to taste, and add 1 cup water, and lemon juice, and pour over grape leaves in pot. Top with several grape leaves and pieces. Invert a plate about the diameter of the pot on top of grape leaves to keep them firmly in place. Cover pot.

~ Bring to boil over high heat, then cook covered very slowly for about 1 hour. Add more water if needed. Steam until grape leaves are soft and are pierced and cut easily with a fork. Do not overcook. The leaves should not fall apart.

~ Cold rolled stuffed grape leaves can be reheated by steaming briefly, or eaten cold.

~ If grape leaves are cooked in shallow pot, they can be turned right on to platter forming a mold. If not, remove and place on platter by hand, dipping fingers in water to cool off.

TIME: 1 hour 35 minutes.   SERVES: 8.

ROLLED STUFFED CABBAGE (Yabrak Malfoof)

Another favorite Middle Eastern dish. It does require a little tender loving effort, but the reward is in the eating. It can be prepared ahead.

1 head of green or white cabbage
¾ cup uncooked long grain rice, preferably brown
1/8 teaspoon cinnamon
3 large garlic cloves
3 lemons
2 cups water

2 pounds of lamb meat (boned leg of lamb, fat removed)
1 tomato chopped in small pieces
3 tablespoons fresh dried mint

~ Dip cabbage in boiling water for only 2 minutes, enough to separate the leaves of the cabbage easily.

~ Grind lamb meat with coarse blade. Mix with rice and chopped tomato, seasoning with salt, pepper and cinnamon.

~ Arrange each cabbage leaf on work table (cut if necessary to facilitate rolling up). Put a tablespoon of stuffing, the size of a little finger, on each leaf, at least a half-inch from edge to permit rolling up the leaf. You may need more or less filling depending on the size of the leaf.

~ Start to roll, then fold right side inward and then the left side. Roll up tightly, and then squeeze in hand to seal closed. Roll up as many cabbage leaves as the filling permits.

~ Place about 4-6 unused cabbage leaves on bottom of 5 quart pot. Neatly stack rolled cabbage leaves in the pot.

~ Pound garlic with mint and dash of salt, and add juice from one lemon. Pour over rolled cabbage in pot. Add two cups of water to permit cabbage to steam. Top with a few unused cabbage leaves.

~ Invert a plate (with a diameter just smaller than the pot) over the cabbage. Cover pot.

~ Bring to boil over high heat. Lower heat and cook slowly for about 30 minutes. Add juice from 2 lemons. Cook another 30 minutes or until cabbage leaf is cut easily with fork. Serve on platter with Laban.

TIME: 1½ hours.   SERVES: 6.

ZUCCHINI OR SUMMER SQUASH WITH LAMB (Koosa mu'a Luhm)

This resembles an omelet with many ingredients, and is especially tasty for an easy lunch.

1 pound lamb meat (boned leg of lamb, fat removed)
2 medium onions
3-4 squash (zucchini or yellow summer)
4 eggs
2-3 fresh tomatoes

~ Grind the lamb meat coarsely with the onion. Sauté them in saucepan for about 10 minutes until the meat is almost done and no pink can be seen.

~ Cut squash and tomatoes into small pieces, and mix with lamb in saucepan. Stir and cover, cooking over low heat for 5 minutes.

~ Add one beaten egg for each person served with salt and pepper. Cook for a few minutes, then stir, and cook over low heat for about 5 more minutes.

TIME: ½ hour.   SERVES: 4.

ABLAMA

This is a favorite of everybody. Stuffed squash is wonderful served with laban on the side. Easy on the digestive system.

1 dozen small fat green squash 2 inches long
2 teaspoons fresh dried mint
1-1½ pounds lamb meat
5-6 ripe tomatoes
½ teaspoon cinnamon (or to taste)
¼ teaspoon cumin

2-3 garlic cloves
2 cups water
1 small onion
½ cup pine nuts (or to taste)

~ Core the squash.

~ Pound garlic, mint and salt; add water.

~ Wash squash and rinse the inside well with the water mixture; save the water for cooking stage.

PREPARE THE FILLING

~ Mince lamb meat and onion, seasoning with salt, pepper and cinnamon. Add pine nuts.

~ Fill the squash ¾ full or almost to the end. Arrange squash in shallow pan and bake with tomato sauce.

PREPARE TOMATO SAUCE

~ Cut tomatoes into small pieces. Add dash of salt and the water mixture in which the squash was rinsed. Cook well under slow heat until soft. Strain the tomatoes over the stuffed squash.

~ Bake in 350° F oven until done. Do not preheat the oven.

TIME: 45 minutes.   SERVES: 6.

LAMB WITH ASPARAGUS

This simple dish makes a very good lunch or supper.

1 pound asparagus
½ pound lamb meat (boned leg of lamb, fat removed)
2 garlic cloves
2 medium onions
2 tablespoons olive oil
3 eggs
¼ teaspoon ground coriander seeds

~ Wash asparagus and cut into 1½ inch lengths, removing hard stem.

~ Place asparagus in boiling water with 1 teaspoon salt. Boil the water for a minute. Remove from heat and discard water.

~ Chop lamb coarsely. Saute in olive oil in stew pot with sliced garlic and onion for about 10 minutes, until tender.

~ Add asparagus, season with coriander and salt and pepper, and cook for 8-10 minutes until tender.

~ Just before serving, add beaten eggs to the hot meat and asparagus. Mix together well and cook with pot covered for 15 minutes.

TIME: 45 minutes.   SERVES: 3 - 5.

LAMB KAFTAS (PATTIES) WITH VEGETABLES

When my grandchildren were small they sometimes asked why they couldn't have regular hamburgers like other children. Although kafta uses ground meat it is less fatty and more spicy and succulent than hamburger, and now that my grandchildren have had hamburgers, they really appreciate it. Kaftas are also delicious served with just rice.

3 pounds lamb (boned leg of lamb, fat removed)
2 medium onions
½ stalk of celery
5 fresh tomatoes
2 teaspoons of butter
Few shakes of cayenne pepper

1 cup raw wheat germ
2 egg yolks
3-4 garlic cloves
1 bunch carrots
½ cup cooking red wine
1 pound fresh peas (or frozen

~ Grind lamb meat with fine blade. Mix with raw wheat germ. Add 2 egg yolks and season with salt and pepper, mixing well. Form into small kaftas (round shaped patties).

~ Broil kaftas in oven until brown on slightly greased pan.

~ In a stewing pot, sauté in butter sliced onion, garlic, peeled carrots, celery and tomatoes cut into pieces over medium heat, until half done.

~ Add wine and cayenne pepper.

~ Add kaftas to the hot vegetables and cook over low flame for half an hour.

~ Cook peas in a separate pot until barely done (a few minutes for frozen peas, about 10 minutes for fresh peas).

~ Serve vegetable mixture on a large platter (1-2 inches in depth), circling the platter with rice, (p. 146) and putting the kafta on top of the vegetables and the peas on top of the kafta.

TIME: 1 hour 15 minutes.   SERVES: 8.

BEEF KAFTAS (PATTIES) WITH PEAS

Kaftas are patties shaped oblong or round. They are made with lean beef and broiled. The sauted vegetables add zest to the meal.

2 pounds lean beef
3 large garlic cloves
1 pound shelled fresh peas (or
  1 pound frozen peas)

6 medium onions
3 medium fresh tomatoes
1 tablespoon olive oil
Herbs of choice

~ Grind the meat with 2 onions, season with salt and pepper to taste, and mix well.

~ Form meat into small kaftas. Make small meat ball, then roll in palms of hands into oblong or round patties, 2 inches in diameter by 3 inches long.

~ Broil until brown (about 12 minutes) on pan lightly greased with olive oil.

~ In large skillet, sauté 4 sliced onions and garlic in 1 tablespoon of olive oil for 5 minutes over medium heat. Add tomatoes cut in chunks and salt and pepper to taste. Sauté for another 10 minutes.

~ Add fresh peas and sauté just until peas are barely cooked, about 5-8 minutes. (If frozen peas are used, saute only about 4 minutes).

~ To serve, place sautéed vegetables in middle of large platter about 1-2 inches deep. Circle cooked rice around sauted vegetables. Place the kaftas on the top of the vegetables.

TIME: 45 minutes.   SERVES: 6.

BEEF WITH WINE

This is a simple, quick dish with an enticing low-fat sauce.

2 pounds lean beef (or lamb)
2 tablespoons white vinegar
7 large garlic cloves
Herbs of choice

2 cups red cooking wine
7-9 small white onions
1 tablespoon olive oil

~ Slice meat in 4 inch lengths and one inch widths. In a glass or china container, marinate meat with wine and vinegar for 1 hour (the marinade should just about cover the meat).

~ Remove meat from marinade (which is reserved), and broil it for a few minutes on each side, until slightly browned.

~ On top of stove, saute sliced onions and garlic with olive oil over low heat in covered pan until soft, about 10 minutes. Then season with salt and pepper.

~ Place meat in a covered baking pot. Pour a little marinade over the onions to capture the contents. Then add onions and all the marinade to the meat.

~ Bake in 350° F oven, testing after 30 minutes for tenderness. Fork should insert easily into the meat.

~ Serve with rice or baked potato and steamed vegetables.

TIME: 2 hours.   SERVES: 6.

BURGHUL FALFAL (Ground Lamb and Cracked Wheat)

This low fat, high energy dish is simple to make and easy to eat. With lots of garlic, it is highly flavorful. The lamb broth gives the dish a magnificent taste.

1 pound lamb meat (boned leg of lamb, fat removed)
6-7 garlic cloves
2 cups coarse burghul #3
4 cups water or lamb broth

~ Mince lamb meat. Season with salt and pepper, and sauté over low heat with garlic cut into pieces for about 10 minutes, until lamb is partially cooked.

~ Add burghul, mix well, and over low heat sauté for 5 minutes, stirring frequently.

~ Cover with 4 cups of water or broth made from lamb bones (p. 50) until the liquid is 4 inches above the lamb/burghul mixture. Cook like rice until done (the burghul should be fluffy).

~ Serve with laban.

TIME: 45 minutes.   SERVES: 6 - 8.

STUFFED POTATOES

I like this recipe especially on a cold, winter day. It is appetizing and gives off a soothing warmth in the eating.

6 large smooth potatoes
1 medium onion
3 fresh tomatoes
4 tablespoons olive oil or ¼ cup
  of vegetable oil spread

1½ pounds lamb meat
4 tablespoons pine nuts
2 large onions

~ Wash, peel and core potatoes ready for lamb stuffing.

PREPARE THE STUFFING

~ Mince lamb meat with 1 medium onion; season with salt and pepper. Add pine nuts and cook until medium done.

~ Stuff potatoes with filling.

~ Place potatoes on tray greased with 1 tablespoon olive oil and broil until pink on top.

PREPARE SAUCE

~ Cut the tomatoes into small chunks, slice 2 large onions and saute until medium done, using 3 tablespoons olive oil or ¼ cup vegetable oil spread.

~ Arrange potatoes in roasting pan with sauce on the bottom of the roasting pan.

~ Cover and bake at 350° F for 25 minutes, until potatoes are done but not overdone.

TIME: 1½ hours.   SERVES: 6.

MAIN DISHES
WITH VEGETABLES

VEGETABLE CASSEROLE

This dish looks like a custard and can be served as a vegetable with meat or with fish, or by itself for a light lunch or supper.

3 medium carrots
½ cup coarsely chopped
   celery with leaves
½ cup milk
1 teaspoon basil

2 medium onion or 4 scallions with tops
½ bunch parsley
2 cups kale
4 eggs slightly beaten

~ Grind all raw vegetables very fine in a meat grinder, or cut in a food processor.

~ Add remaining ingredients and mix thoroughly.

~ Pour into a well-greased (with butter) 9x12 glass or stainless steel pan.

~ Set pan in a larger pan of hot water and bake in a 350° F oven (not preheated) for 75 minutes until set.

TIME: 1 hour 45 minutes.   SERVES: 8 - 10.

BURGHUL WITH SWISS CHARD OR CHICORY LETTUCE

This recipe can be served with a tossed salad. Or one can put laban over the serving. It is a satisfying and nourishing light meal, and can be prepared quickly as with similar hearty dishes. Cayenne pepper adds its distinctive zest and I like using it here.

3 medium onions	3 garlic cloves
¾ cup olive oil	1 cup coarse burghul #3
1 cup water or lamb broth	1 bunch swiss chard or large head
½ teaspoon cayenne pepper	of chicory lettuce

~ Slice onions and garlic and saute slightly in olive oil in covered 3 quart pot.

~ After washing thoroughly and draining, chop the chard or chicory into small pieces and add to onions and garlic without mixing. Let them cook until the greens have reduced somewhat.

~ Add the burghul and cook 5-6 minutes without mixing.

~ Mix all together and add one cup water or one cup lamb broth.

~ Season with salt and cayenne (or black) pepper and cook slowly, until done. The dish should be moist when finished.

~ Serve on platter.

TIME: ½ hour.   SERVES: 6.

BLACKEYED PEAS

A hearty simple dish that sticks to the ribs.

1 pound blackeyed peas
3 good size onions
4 garlic cloves
½ cup brown rice or coarse burghul #3
¼ cup olive oil

~ Wash peas and rice and put them in a pot. Add sliced onions, garlic, olive oil and water, or combination water and lamb broth to cover peas and then 2 inches above that point.

~ Cook using medium heat and, if needed, add more water. The consistency should be like a stew, not like a soup.

TIME: 55 minutes.   SERVES: 10.

'MDARDARA (Lentils with Rice and Scallions)

This simple dish is rich in iron, delicious, and very filling. It makes an attractive centerpiece for a basic meal.

¾ pound lentils
½ cup long grain rice, brown preferred, or coarse burghul #3
6 medium or 3 large onions
½ cup olive oil
¼ teaspoon cinnamon
3 cups cold water
6 large radishes
1 bunch of scallions

~ Slice and sauté onions in olive oil in 5 quart pot until soft and slightly browned. Remove and set aside one-half of onions.

~ Wash lentils and rice in a bowl with cold water. Rinse several times and drain.

~ Add lentils, rice, salt, pepper, cinnamon and water to onions in pot. Bring to boil over high heat. Then reduce to moderate/low heat and cook until dry and fluffy, but not well done, about 40 minutes.

~ Place 'Mdardara on platter, put reserved sautéed onions on top, mince scallions and sprinkle over the top, and place halved radishes evenly spaced around the bottom edge of lentil mound for decoration.

TIME: 55 minutes - 1 hour.   SERVES: 8.

'MJADARA (Lentils with Rice and Onions)

This dish is similar to 'Mdardara.

1 pound lentils
1 cup long grain rice (preferably brown) or coarse burghul #3
3 medium or 2 large onions
¼ cup olive oil
¼ teaspoon cinnamon
5½ cups water
Dash of vinegar (optional)

~ Slice and sauté onions in 5 quart pot in olive oil until slightly brown and soft.

~ Wash lentils, rice or burghul in cold water and drain.

~ Put all lentils, rice or burghul, salt, pepper, cinnamon and water in pot, bring to boil with high heat, then lower to medium/low heat.

~ Cook on slow heat until well done.

~ If you wish, you can simply put all ingredients except rice or burghul in pot to cook, then add rice or burghul when half cooked.

~ Serve with a dash of vinegar if you like a zesty touch.

TIME: 1 hour.   SERVES: 8 - 10.

ROLLED GRAPE LEAVES WITH CHICK PEAS

This dish takes some time and care to roll the leaves without splitting them. When finished, the piled rolls look very elegant.

½ cup chick peas
¼ cup long grain brown rice
2 medium onions
2-3 lemons
1 pound grape leaves
½ cup olive oil

~ Soak chick peas overnight in water, first removing small stone and blemished chick peas. The next day wash thoroughly and grind with onions into small pieces, using preferably a hand grinder. Add uncooked rice, lemon juice and olive oil. Season with salt and pepper and mix the ingredients well.

~ Place grape leaves in boiling water and lift out immediately.

~ Remove stems and then roll the grape leaves, using 1 teaspoon of filling for each leaf.

~ Line the bottom of the pot with torn grape leaves (not usable for rolling) and place rolled grape leaves evenly in rows and layers. Place 2 or 3 grape leaves on top and then place a dish upside down firmly over the contents.

~ Cook slowly until done. The rolled grape leaf should be firm, not mushy.

~ Arrange rolled grape leaves in a pleasing design on a platter.

TIME: 1 hour.   SERVES: 4 - 6.

BAKED SQUASH OMELET

This is a good recipe for young college students because it can be made rather quickly and has nutrition an active young person needs.

4 medium zucchini
1 cup water
1 cup fine burghul #1
½ cup pure olive oil (light variety)
4 eggs
2 bunches of parsley (or one big bunch) minced
4 bunches scallions chopped

~ Wash and clean squash well (do not peel). Cut into pieces and place in 3 quart pot.

~ Add a few grains of salt and cook the squash in the water until they are soft enough to mash. Then mash them in the remaining water.

~ Remove from heat, add burghul to the cooked squash and allow to soak for 5 minutes.

~ Add olive oil, season with salt and pepper and mix together.

~ Beat eggs and add to the squash. Add minced parsley and chopped scallions. Mix well all together with spoon.

~ Put squash/egg mixture in a 14x9 glass baking pan and bake in 350° F oven (not preheated) for 1 hour.

~ Cut into squares to serve.

TIME: 1½ hours.   SERVES: 6 - 8.

RICE WITH ZUCCHINI

Another simple satisfying dish. The cayenne pepper gives it a feisty flavor.

3 medium onions
3 garlic cloves
¾ cup olive oil
3 large zucchini
1 cup long grain brown rice
1 cup water or lamb broth
½ teaspoon cayenne pepper

~ Slice onions and garlic and sauté them slightly in olive oil in covered 3 quart pot.

~ Slice zucchini and mix with rice that has been thoroughly washed. Add to onions and garlic.

~ Add water or lamb broth and cook until done, seasoning with salt and cayenne pepper.

TIME: 1 hour.   SERVES: 6.

KIBBI WITH POTATOES (Kibbit Batata)

Children like this recipe because it's easy to eat, and I like it for them because it is nutritious too.

5 large potatoes
2 large onions
1 cup walnuts
2 cups fine burghul #1
¼ cup olive oil

~ Boil potatoes, do not overcook.

~ Grind together potatoes, onions and walnuts.

~ Cover burghul with water and then squeeze the water out.

~ Mix in the burghul with above and grind again.

~ Make into patties or in 3 inch squares.

~ Bake in 350° F oven, until brown.

TIME: 1 hour.   SERVES: 6.

CHICK PEAS AND LABAN ON TOAST

My granddaughter used to eat this dish for breakfast. She said it got her through the day and saved her money at lunch besides.

1½ cups dried chick peas
1 quart laban
3 garlic cloves
2 tablespoons fresh dried mint (or to taste)
1 red bell pepper
6 slices of whole wheat bread

~ Soak chick peas (removing small stones and blemished peas) overnight in water; then wash well the next morning.

~ Cover peas with water in pot and cook until done, under medium heat.

~ Toast slices of whole wheat bread and place in a spacious bowl. Use the water in which the chick peas were cooked to soak the toasted bread.

~ Put chick peas on top of the toasted bread.

~ Pound garlic, mint and salt together, mix with laban and pour over the chick peas to cover.

~ Garnish top with red bell pepper and serve.

TIME: 45 minutes.   SERVES: 6.

MAIN DISHES
WITH FISH

FISH WITH VEGETABLES

An efficient meal in one, just make a salad and you've got dinner.

1 bunch celery	4 carrots (scraped)
2 green peppers	3 medium onions
2 garlic cloves	2 teaspoons butter
3 fresh tomatoes	6 pieces of white fish, (for example, scrod,
2 tablespoons olive oil	cod, flounder)
2 fresh lemons	½ teaspoon paprika

~ Cut in small pieces celery, carrots, green pepper, onions and garlic. Sauté in butter in covered pot to retain liquid. Cook until barely soft.

~ Add tomatoes cut in chunks and cook 10 minutes more.

~ While vegetables are cooking, place fish in pan greased with olive oil. Sprinkle lemon juice, paprika, salt and pepper on top.

~ Broil fish for about 5 minutes, until half done. Immediately lower oven to 250° F.

~ Add vegetables on top of fish and bake (not broil) for about 20 minutes in slow, 250° F oven. Keep juice adequate. Do not let fish dry out. Add water if needed.

TIME: 1 hour.   SERVES: 6.

BAKED FISH WITH SPICES AND TARATOR SAUCE

Baked fish with tarator is a rich and elegant way to prepare fish for a special evening. Colorful vegetables add to the presentation.

2 pounds white fish (for example, flounder, scrod, fillet of sole)
2 lemons
1/8 teaspoon tarragon or curry powder
Parsley to garnish

~ Slice lemons and arrange slices on bottom of baking dish.

~ Place fish on top and season with salt, pepper, and either tarragon or curry powder.

~ Bake in 350° F oven for no more than 10 minutes until flakey. Place on platter and serve immediately with tarator sauce (see below) and garnish with parsley.

TARATOR SAUCE

2-3 garlic cloves
¼ cup tahini
2 tablespoons cold water
2 lemons

~ Pound garlic with salt. Add tahini and lemon juice and mix. Add cold water as needed and mix until smooth. Taste should be a little bit tart.

~ Serve over warm fish.

~ Alternatively, use a blender to blend garlic, salt, lemon juice and water. When that is smooth, blend in tahini for just a few seconds.

TIME: 20 minutes.   SERVES: 4 - 6.

FISH WITH WHEAT GRAIN (Kibbit Samak)

This version of Kibbi is made with fish, an enticing approach to fish.

6-7 slices of white fish (cod, scrod, 7 medium onions
   flounder, sole, halibut) 4 garlic cloves
1 cup fine burghul #1 1 teaspoon saffron
1/8 cup olive oil ½ cup olive oil
2-3 lemons

~ Grind with fine blade boned raw white fish with 4 onions and garlic.

~ Wash burghul, squeeze out water, and add to fish. Season with salt and white pepper. Add grated lemon rind. This mixture is called Kibbit Samak. Mix it well by hand.

~ Slice 3 onions. Season with salt and pepper and add 1 teaspoon saffron. Mix with 1/8 cup of olive oil.

~ Put this onion mixture at the bottom of a shallow glass pan. Spread Kibbit Samak on top. Pat it down, using a handful of water sprinkled on the Kibbi to make it smooth.

~ Cut the Kibbit Samak into diamond shapes with diagonal cuts across the dish.

~ Spread about ¼ cup of olive oil on top, and bake until brown in 300° F oven for 35 minutes, or until done.

~ Wait 10 minutes after removing from the oven before serving.

TIME: About 1 hour. SERVES: 6.

VEGETABLES

STRING BEANS WITH OLIVE OIL (Loubieh bi Zayt)

This dish goes well with fish or served cold by itself on a hot summer day.

2 pounds string beans
2 medium onions
7 garlic cloves
2 medium tomatoes
¼ cup olive oil

~ Remove ends of beans, break in half and wash.

~ Slice onions and garlic; sauté lightly in olive oil and then put the string beans on top.

~ Cut tomatoes in small chunks or pieces and place over the string beans. Season with salt and pepper.

~ Cook for 10 minutes slowly, then mix all the ingredients and continue cooking slowly, until tender.

TIME: 50 minutes.   SERVES: 6 if side dish, 4 if by itself.

EGGPLANT WITH LEMON, OLIVE OIL AND GARLIC

This makes a delicious side dish.

3 medium eggplants
2-3 lemons
3 garlic cloves
2-3 tablespoons olive oil

~ Bake eggplant in shallow pan in 400° F oven after scoring or pricking the eggplant to allow steam to escape. Bake until eggplant is cooked but still firm.

~ Peel the skin and cut eggplant into chunks.

~ Prepare the dressing

~ Pound garlic with salt, to taste. Add olive oil and lemon juice.

~ Mix eggplant with dressing and serve.

TIME: 40 minutes.   SERVES: 7 - 8.

BEET LEAVES OR SWISS CHARD WITH OLIVE OIL AND ONIONS

This recipe can be served as a side dish with an entree or as lunch when accompanied with boiled potatoes coarsely mashed and seasoned with salt and pepper, basil and a little olive oil. Besides a wonderful taste, beet leaves or red swiss chard bring color to the table.

3 large bunches of beet leaves
4 onions
5-6 garlic cloves
¼ cup olive oil

~ Cut beet leaves in small pieces and in 2 inch lengths on stem.

~ Wash them well with warm water and salt until all sand is out. Put in colander and drain well.

~ Slice onion and garlic and sauté in olive oil.

~ Add the beet leaves with stems and cook on low heat until done, about 10 minutes. Turn over once after leaves have reduced some. Do not overcook.

~ Serve in a bowl.

TIME: 20 minutes.   SERVES: 6 if side dish, 4 if served with potatoes for lunch.

BEETS WITH ONIONS AND OLIVE OIL

This dish has an enticing taste when served warm and refreshing when served cold in summertime. The onions provide enough seasoning, making it unneccesary to use salt.

10 beets
2 medium red onions
Olive oil to taste
½ teaspoon tarragon (optional)

~ Cook beets until done but firm. Cut into crescent shaped pieces. Slice onions, add to beets and mix all with olive oil.

SERVES: 4.

STEAMED BROCCOLI WITH GARLIC, LEMON AND OLIVE OIL

An elegant vegetable. Its taste and deep green color add a distinctive touch, especially when served with fish. When served as part of a meal of vegetables, it holds its own.

~ Steam 3 bunches of broccoli, removing the hard part of the stalk and leaving good-sized florets intact. Pound 3 large garlic cloves with several dashes of salt. Add the juice of 3-4 lemons or to taste and about 3 tablespoons of olive oil.

~ To serve, dip each floret in the garlic, lemon and oil mixture and place on platter. When finished, pour whatever remains over the entire platter.

SERVES: 6 - 8.

STEAMED CAULIFLOWER WITH TARATOR SAUCE

Gives a tantalizing taste to any meal. Good with fish dishes or as part of a meal of vegetables.

~ Steam 1 large head of cauliflower after separating into sizable florets. Always keep vegetables on the firm side. Dip in Tarator Sauce (p. 113) and serve on platter.

~ Garnish with parsley.

SERVES: 4.

FAVA BEANS WITH OLIVE OIL (Foole)

A filling side dish or even a basic lunch.

~ Soak in cold water 1 pound dried fava beans overnight and one whole day. Wash them and cook them until soft and succulent. Pound 4-5 garlic cloves and add the juice of 2 lemons. Mix with fava beans, adding ½ cup olive oil. Season with salt and pepper. Or you can let people add their own oil.

SERVES: 4 - 6.

DESSERTS

MA'MOOL (Pastry filled with Crushed Pistachio Nuts)

Ma'mool is an exquisite light pastry filled with pistachios. Not to be made when you are in a hurry.

INGREDIENTS FOR DOUGH

2 cups baby farina or semolina (fine flour)

1 cup warm milk

1 jigger brandy (or whiskey)

1¼ teaspoons mahlab

1 tablespoon orange blossom water
  (or rose water)

1¼ pound clarified butter

1 yeast cake (2 tablespoons)

4 cups unbleached white
  flour

INGREDIENTS FOR FILLING

1 pound unsalted pistachio (some use black walnuts) or ½ pound of each
  (pistachios alone are preferred)

1 cup sugar

2½ tablespoons orange blossom water or rose water

PREPARE DOUGH

~ Mix butter and farina the night before cooking. Use unsalted butter or clarify butter to remove salt. I prefer clarified butter because it is purer. Boil very gently and stir until there is no more foam on top. Salt will sink to bottom of pan. Strain the butter through a fine strainer over the farina. Stir and leave over night. This dough does not rise.

~ Beat farina/butter mixture for about 10 minutes until it turns creamy white. Add brandy and mahlab.

~ Dissolve yeast in warm milk, stirring. Add to farina mixture. Gradually add the flour to the mixture, mixing until the dough is smooth.

PREPARE THE FILLING

~ Grind the pistachios coarse. Mix with sugar and orange blossom water.

ASSEMBLING THE MA'MOOL

~ Take a small amount of dough and round it in the cradle of the hand. With the forefinger, core into the dough until it is in the shape of a small, oval cup with thin sides. The ma'mool is more delicious if it has lots of filling. This is feasible if the cored hole is large and the sides of the cup are thin.

~ Insert about a teaspoon of filling into the cup, and then gently close the opening with thumb and other fingers, face the closed opening into palm of hand and finish rounding.

~ Decorate top of ma'mool by pinching the soft dough with a pastry crimper or tweezers, again and again until the effect is one groove after another. A cookie mold designed to be gently pressed on the top can alternatively be used.

~ Bake in preheated 300° F oven about 40 minutes, or until brown on the bottom and barely showing color on the top.

~ Sprinkle superfine powdered sugar on top of the hot ma'mool.

Makes about 80 ma'mool.

MACAROON KASHAB (Glazed Sesame Seed Macaroon)

Although macaroons may be considered sweets, they serve as nourishment also. The macaroons themselves are not sweet, but the glaze balances the subtle tastes in the body of the macaroon.

INGREDIENTS FOR MACAROONS

1 or 2 cakes of yeast (2 for quicker results)
10 cups unbleached white flour
5 eggs
2½ cups olive oil
4 tablespoons anise
1 tablespoon orange blossom water

1 cup cold milk
2 cups sesame seeds
  (optional: slightly toasted in
  oven)
1 tablespoons mahlab

INGREDIENTS FOR SYRUP

5 cups white sugar
Juice of 2 lemons

1½ cups cold water
1½ tablespoons orange
  blossom water

PREPARE THE MACAROON

~ Dissolve yeast cakes in cold milk. Stir to dissolve well.

~ In a large bowl, mix unbleached white flour, and sesame seed. Thoroughly blend anise and mahlab in a blender together and add to the bowl.

~ Add olive oil and beaten eggs to flour mixture.

~ Knead all the ingredients well (but not hard) for about 15 minutes until the bowl is clean on the sides. The dough should be a little loose.

~ Cover and let the dough rise well for 1 hour.

~ After the dough has risen, form two hands full into a big, long rounded shape on the work table, about 2 feet long. Cut the dough into 1 inch pieces.

~ To form macaroon, press each 1 inch piece gently against a flat cheese grater against the grain to get a pattern on the macaroon. Gently remove the dough from the grater in one motion with the ends of your fingers, rolling the dough to form a rolled macaroon (it should be about the shape of a forefinger). Place onto cookie sheet, with the overlap end of the macaroon resting against the cookie sheet (thus the overlap will be at the bottom of the macaroon).

~ Bake at 400° F for about 25 minutes. The macaroons are finished when slightly brown.

PREPARE SYRUP FOR GLAZE

~ Dissolve sugar and water. Add lemon juice. Bring to boil stirring constantly. Let the mixture boil 3-4 minutes. Add mazaher (orange blossom water).

~ With a slotted spoon, dip cooked macaroons in hot syrup to glaze as soon as they are removed from the oven. Remove from glaze to a colander sitting in a larger bowl to permit the macaroon to drain slightly before being placed on a platter.

~ If macaroons are being stored for future eating, use wax paper between layers to prevent them from sticking to each other.

TIME: 4 hours.   MAKES: about 92 macaroons.

NAMOURA

Another nourishing sweet that children like to pick up and run with at snack time or with tea.

2 cups semolina or farina	1 tablespoon butter
2 cups sugar	2 cups laban
1 teaspoon baking soda	1 cup coconut
72 blanched almonds	2 tablespoons Tahini

~ Grease baking pan (9x13) well with tahini to avoid sticking.

~ Put all ingredients together in a bowl and work until the batter is smooth.

~ Spread smoothly in pan.

~ Place blanched almonds about 8 across to cover the surface of the pan.

~ Bake in 250° F oven for 1 hour.

~ Let the namoura cool and pour cup of maple syrup over the pan

~ With a wet sharp knife, gently cut the namoura with evenly spaced diagonal lines across the longer end of the pan and then along the shorter end, to create diamond shaped pieces. Cut with an up and down motion, as in cutting a cake, to avoid disturbing the surface.

TIME: 1 hour 15 minutes.   MAKES: 36 pieces.

KA'AK (A Sweet Yeast Bread)

Ka'ak are tasty and nutritious whether eaten with coffee or tea in the morning or as a snack with milk. I make them by the dozens, and they disappear by the dozens!

1 yeast cake
12 cups unbleached white flour
4 teaspoons anise seed
1 pound clarified butter

1 quart milk
2 teaspoons mahlab
5 eggs

~ Dissolve yeast in cold milk. Then add flour, and mahlab and anise seed which have been blended in the blender until they are powder-like.

~ To clarify, boil the butter until there is no foam on the top and then strain the butter over the flour mixture. Add the unbeaten eggs (I use the egg whites and less of the yolks). Mix all and knead well. Let rise.

~ To make the ka'ak, take a handful of dough, and roll it out with your hands until dough is elongated and about 1½ inches thick. Cut in pieces and form into doughnut shape. Using a thimble, impress each ka'ak in a braided pattern so that the hole doesn't close up in baking. The dough has an elastic quality, and this can happen.

~ Bake in 400° F oven, 20 minutes, or until golden brown on bottom.

TO PREPARE GLAZE

2 cups milk
Powdered sugar

3 tablespoons rose water

~ Glaze top of ka'ak using a mixture of milk and rose water. Then with your fingers pat powdered sugar over the top.

TIME: 2½ hours.   MAKES: about 90 ka'aks.

STUFFED HONEY DEW

You can't lose with good ingredients.

1 Honey Dew	2 packages unflavored gelatin
¾ cup brown sugar	2-3 lemons
2 grapefruit	4 oranges
1½ cup cold water	1 package cream cheese

~ Peel and core the honey dew, taking the fruit out in the form of melon balls.

PREPARE GELATIN

~ Boil water, and pour over gelatin and brown sugar. Mix well and cool some until the mixture begins to gel.

~ Juice lemon, grapefruit and oranges and add to the gelatin, mixing well. You can also mix in the melon balls.

~ Put gelatin mixture in the shell of the honey dew and refrigerate.

PREPARE TOPPING

~ Cream the cream cheese until it is soft.

~ When gelatin is firm, cover the outside of the honey dew with the cream cheese and slice for serving.

TIME: 40 minutes.   SERVES: 5 - 6.

HALAWA BI JIBNEY (Sweet Cheese Pudding)

Sweet cheese pudding is a nice dessert after a light meal.

1½ cups farina
¼ cup butter
¾ cup sugar
1/8 cup cold water
Few drops fresh lemon juice
1 pound jibney (cheese) (p. 149)

~ Melt the butter over low heat and add the farina. Keep stirring until the farina is light in color.

PREPARE THE SYRUP

~ Combine sugar and a little cold water in a pot and cook. Stir continuously until the mixture comes to a medium boil. Add a few drops of fresh lemon juice.

~ Add this syrup to the mixture of butter and farina and stir well until you achieve a dough-like mixture. The consistency becomes thick very quickly.

~ Slice cheese and add to above while on a very low fire and mix well.

~ Serve hot.

TIME: 40 minutes.   SERVES: 4 - 6.

PARFAIT

An easy dessert requiring lots of fresh juices

3 packages unflavored gelatin
1 cup brown sugar
2 cups water
2-3 lemons
2 grapefruit
4 oranges
1 pint vanilla ice cream

PREPARE GELATIN

~ Boil water and pour over gelatin and brown sugar.

~ Add juices of lemons, grapefruit, and oranges.

~ Gel in refrigerator until firm.

PREPARE PARFAIT

~ Mix gelatin with vanilla ice cream in blender.

~ Serve in parfait glasses and refrigerate until time to serve.

TIME: 20 minutes.   SERVES: 8.

CREAM CHEESE GELATIN DELIGHT

Everyone waits for this at Christmas once a year. I also serve it on other special occasions.

5 packages unflavored gelatin	1 cup cold water
1 cup hot water	1½ cup dark brown sugar
4 lemons	6 oranges
3 grapefruits	2 large packages cream cheese
2 cans sliced pineapples	

~ Dissolve well unflavored gelatin with cold water.

~ Add hot water and dissolve well.

~ Add brown sugar and stir well.

~ Juice lemons, oranges, and grapefruit.

~ Add citrus juice unstrained and stir all well.

~ Pour into bowl and gel well in refrigerator overnight. The gel should be very firm.

~ Mix gelatin, cream cheese and sliced pineapple in blender (first set on chop and then set on purée) in small amounts until all have been blended.

~ Fold in cake pan (10 inch in diameter with tube in middle) and gel well one day before serving.

~ Turn the dessert onto a platter. This takes quick but steady movements so the dessert slips onto the platter without breaking up.

~ Decorate with fresh strawberries in the opening at the center and over the entire top of the dessert.

~ Slice and serve as one would a cake.

SERVES: 20.

APPLE CAKE

This apple cake recipe leaves a taste superior to apple pie because it is lighter.

INGREDIENTS FOR DOUGH

¼ cup butter
1 cup brown sugar
1 lemon peel
Dash of salt

2 eggs
2 lemons
1 cup unbleached white flour

INGREDIENTS FOR FILLING

30 tart apples
1 cup brown sugar
¼ teaspoon mace
1 egg

2 lemons
2 teaspoons cinnamon
1 tablespoon butter
¼ teaspoon mace

PREPARE THE DOUGH

~ Cream butter and then add eggs, sugar, lemon juice, lemon peel, flour and dash of salt.

~ Mix and knead the mixture well.

~ Divide the dough into two parts.

~ Roll one part very thin on the worktable putting flour underneath. Use large pan (18x11x2) and spread a very thin layer of the dough.

~ Bake this layer in preheated 400° F oven for 7 minutes until it is a little brown.

PREPARE THE FILLING

~ Peel apples and slice them thinly.

~ Mix the apples with lemon juice, brown sugar, cinnamon, mace and butter at room temperature.

~ Spread over the baked crust.

~ Spread the second layer of dough over the apples evenly. This requires rolling the dough thinly on the worktable and then placing it over the apples, continuing the process until all the apples are covered.

~ Beat one egg well and spread it over the top crust.

~ Bake at 350° F until top is brown.

~ Serve plain, with whipped cream, or with vanilla ice cream.

TIME: 1 hour 15 minutes.   SERVES: 20.

CRANBERRY WITH ORANGES AND APPLES

This colorful, festive dessert casserole is always welcome in brisk weather. It is baked and served warm at room temperature. The treat is doubled and more if the fruits are grown organically, producing a most delicious taste.

1 pound cranberries
5 oranges
5 medium apples
¼ cup maple syrup, or to taste
½ teaspoon cardamom (optional)

~ Peel and cut oranges into medium size chunks.

~ Peel and cut apples into medium size chunks.

~ Place one layer of apples in bottom of casserole, then one layer of cranberry followed by one layer of oranges and repeat until finished.

~ Pour maple syrup on top and bake in 350° F oven until done, about 20-25 minutes.

TIME: 55 minutes.   SERVES: 6 - 8.

CHRISTMAS BREAD

Makes Christmas morning a bit special. Something to anticipate.

2 cups fresh orange juice
2-3 cups sugar
1 teaspoon ginger
1 teaspoon nutmeg
8 cups unbleached white flour
3 eggs
1 orange, grated skin
Blanched almonds for garnish

½ cup butter
½ teaspoon salt
1 teaspoon cinnamon
1 cake of yeast, 2 if in a hurry
1 cup chopped walnuts
¾-1 cup mixed fruit or white raisins
½ cup milk

~ Warm orange juice until hot. Do not boil.

~ Pour over room temperature butter, sugar, grated orange, salt and the spices of ginger, cinnamon and nutmeg in large bowl; mix and let cool a bit.

~ Add yeast cake dissolved with cold milk and mix well.

~ Add 3 eggs beaten well and add to mixture.

~ Add ½ flour and mix by hand.

~ Add ¾-1 cup mixed fruit or white raisins to rest of the flour and then add to the total mixture.

~ Knead until mixture is firm, about 10 minutes.

~ Divide to make 2 loaves and let rise in baking bowl.

~ When the dough has risen well, pat firmly and baste with one egg and let the dough rise again.

~ Put in greased pan, cut a pattern on the top of the bread, and and let the dough rise a third time.

~ Garnish with blanched almonds.

~ Bake in preheated oven at 325° F for 20 minutes.

TIME: 55 minutes.   SERVES: 15 - 20.

RICE PUDDING

This is a simple, easy dessert that is satisfying especially if one is under the weather for one reason or another.

1 cup milk
1 cup basmati rice
2 cups water
2 tablespoons sugar
1 teaspoon rose water
1 teaspoon orange water

~ Cook rice with water until rice is done.

~ Add milk, sugar and rose and orange blossom water and cook until creamy.

Serve in individual glass bowls.

TIME: 35 minutes.   SERVES: 8.

TWO-TWO-TWO COOKIES

This easy to remember cookie aims for hearty and nourishing simplicity. It has proven to be a favorite of my family and friends. I use as many organically grown ingredients as possible and this adds to our enjoyment.

2 cups unbleached white flour
1 teaspoon baking powder
2 cups shredded coconut
2 cups raisins
4 egg whites
1 teaspoon orange blossom water

1 teaspoon baking soda
2 cups wheat germ
2 cups walnut, chopped
¼ cup olive oil
1 teaspoon rose water
1/3 cup maple syrup

~ Mix olive oil, eggs white beaten, maple syrup, and rose and orange blossom water.

~ Mix dry ingredients well, then mix these well with the above.

~ Take a spoonful of cookie batter and form the cookies; place on the cookie tin and bake until done in 350° F oven, about 20 minutes.

TIME: 1 hour.   MAKES: about 30 ample cookies.

OATMEAL COOKIES

In New England oatmeal cookies are always welcomed especially with fresh walnuts. Very nice for picnics.

½ cup olive oil
3 tablespoons blackstrap molasses
1 teaspoon lemon juice
3 eggs
1 cup milk
1 pinch of salt
¼ teaspoon mace

1 cup brown sugar
1 teaspoon vanilla
½ teaspoon baking soda
½ cup oatmeal
½ cup unbleached white flour
1 teaspoon cinnamon
½-1 cup chopped walnuts

~ Mix olive oil, brown sugar, molasses and vanilla, or lemon juice. Add eggs well beaten.

~ Combine this mixture with the dry ingredients, oatmeal, flour, salt, cinnamon, mace and walnuts.

~ Mix well and drop cookies with spoon on cookie tray greased with butter.

~ Bake at 350° F oven until brown, about 10-15 minutes.

TIME: 1 hour.   MAKES: 30 ample cookies.

COCONUT, WALNUT AND RAISIN COOKIES

A cookie that also serves as a quick meal if baked in large size.

1 cup unbleached white flour	1 cup wheat germ
1 cup coconut	½ cup chopped walnuts
½ cup raisins	½ cup olive oil
½ cup brown sugar	4 eggs
1-2 tablespoon carob powder	¼ teaspoon mace
Few grains salt	Juice of ½ lemon

~ Mix olive oil and brown sugar well and add eggs well beaten and lemon juice.

~ Combine dry ingredients including walnuts and raisins and fold into liquid mixture and mix well.

~ Grease baking tray with butter.

~ Form cookies by hand and place on tray.

~ Bake in preheated oven at 350° F until done, about 10 minutes.

TIME: 45 minutes.   MAKES: 40 cookies.

SESAME SEED COCONUT COOKIES

Cookies become variations of each other. This is substantial because of the quality of the ingredients.

½ cup olive oil

5 tablespoons carob powder

1 cup unbleached (with skin) sesame
   seeds

Juice of 1 lemon

3 eggs (well beaten)

2 tablespoons brown sugar (if more
   sweetness is desired)

5 tablespoons honey

1 cup coconut

1 teaspoon baking powder

1 pinch salt

2½ cup unbleached white
   flour

~ Place all ingredients in bowl at once and mix well.

~ Grease baking tray with butter.

~ Bake cookies in preheated oven at 350° F, until done, about 10-15 minutes.

TIME: 55 minutes.   MAKES: 30 - 36 cookies.

DATE NUT AND SESAME SEED COOKIES

Yet another version of cookies that are tasty yet stick to your ribs.

2 pounds dates
½ cup unbleached sesame seed
1 teaspoon baking powder
5 eggs
½ cup honey

20 ounce bag of chopped
   walnuts
Few grains of salt
½ cup olive oil
1 cup brown sugar

~ Mix well olive oil, well beaten eggs, sugar and honey.

~ Add flour, dates chopped, walnuts and sesame seed (browned a little in oven) and mix well.

~ Bake cookies on cookie tray until brown in 350° F oven, about 25-30 minutes.

TIME: 45 minutes.   MAKES: 20 cookies.

CARROT COCONUT COOKIES

Another cookie recipe that is a substitute for sugar fillers.

2 cups brown sugar
4 eggs well beaten
2 teaspoons baking powder
1 teaspoon cinnamon
1 cup chopped walnuts
1 cup coconut
1 cup grated carrot or ½ cup,
   as desired

1½ cup olive oil
2 cups whole wheat flour
Few grains of salt
½ teaspoon mace
1 teaspoon lemon juice and grated
   lemon

~ Put ingredients in bowl in above order mix well all together.

~ Grease baking tray with butter.

~ Form cookies by hand and place on tray.

~ Bake in preheated oven at 350° F, until done, about 10 minutes.

TIME: 45 minutes.   MAKES: 30 ample cookies.

SOME BASICS

BREAD

"Eat this bread and you will never spread." Furthermore, it is delicious.

2 cakes yeast (or 2 tablespoons active dry yeast)
2 quarts milk (1 percent milkfat or skim)
5 pounds stone ground whole wheat flour

1. Dissolve yeast in 1 quart cold milk.

2. Add second quart milk warmed to skin temperature and then add flour.

3. Mix well. Knead by alternately pressing with fists and folding the dough until it is smooth and elastic, about 20 minutes. Use the bulk of the dough to pull stray pieces from the sides of the bowl. Dip your hands in milk or water to keep the dough from sticking to them.

4. Let dough rise covered until it has approximately doubled in bulk.

TO BAKE ARABIC BREAD

5. Preheat oven to 500° F with trays inside. For gas ovens, place trays on the bottom of the oven (remove racks). In electric ovens, place trays on the lowest rack.

6. Tear off enough dough to roll into a firm ball about 3½ inches in diameter. Make a total of 10 balls and let them rise on a lightly floured surface for 30 minutes. To keep the balls moist, cover them with a cloth.

7. Cover work surface lightly with flour and rub hands in flour. Using palms and fingers, flatten a ball into a disk about ½ inch thick. Alternatively, you may use a rolling pin. Make sure the edges are thin. Use more flour if dough sticks to work surface. Do not use flour on topside of bread.

8. Drop the disk-shaped loaf onto a hot tray and bake until brown on the bottom (about 6 minutes). Properly made loaves will inflate in the oven.

9. When all 10 loaves are baked, repeat step 6 onward with the remaining dough.

MAKES: about 30 flat loaves.

TO BAKE LOAF BREAD

5. Fashion an amount of dough into an oblong shape that fills a greased loaf pan about two thirds to the top. Make sure the dough is punched down. Let each loaf rise, but not too much. My grandson gives this step about 40 minutes. Use your judgment.

6. Bake all loaves for about 55 minutes in a 350° F oven.

MAKES: 4-5 loaves.

RICE

A satisfying staple accompanying many main dishes. Good by itself in the summer with laban (yogurt) topping the rice.

3 tablespoons butter
20 thin pastas (vermicelli)
2 cups long grain brown rice
4 cups cold water

~ Melt butter in pot, adding the vermicelli in 1 inch lengths, salt to taste, and brown slightly.

~ Add rice, mix well, and sauté slightly. This helps keep rice kernels separate.

~ Add water and let the rice come to a boil.

~ Reduce heat and cook until done. If more water is needed, add just enough to cook the rice. Too much water makes rice soggy, to be avoided.

~ When done, stir once; turn heat off and let the steam do the rest.

TIME: 1 hour.

LABAN (Yogurt)

Laban was a regular part of our diet and remains so. A healthful food used in a variety of recipes, or served by itself at any time.

1 gallon whole or skim milk
4-6 generous tablespoons laban

~ Scald the milk, using high heat, stirring so that it does not stick to the pot.

~ Let it rise to the edge of the pot and take pot away from heat. Cool completely to finger touch, as if testing for baby's milk.

~ Mix the laban starter (4-6 tablespoons laban) with some of the lukewarm milk in a separate bowl, then mix with the rest of the milk.

~ Cover pot and wrap well with towels or place in oven where the pilot keeps the oven warm enough to do the job. Keep 5 or 6 hours or overnight on the kitchen counter or in oven.

~ If after this time, the laban is not quite made, cover again and leave a little longer.

~ Refrigerate until cold. Laban lasts some days in refrigerator. Be sure to keep it covered.

~ Before serving, take a jarful of laban for use as the starter culture for the next time.

MAKES: 3-4 quarts.

FOR THE GRANDCHILDREN

~ Scald the milk and let cool to lukewarm. In a separate cup, put 1 heaping tablespoon laban (to 1 quart of milk) and add some lukewarm milk to mix with the laban starter. Mix in pot, cover and wrap. Keep overnight. In the morning, refrigerate.

LABANEY

Labaney is a spread made from laban which is good with toast in the morning. Labaney can be mixed with fresh dried mint and used as an appetizing dip with olive oil. It is especially good for the children's sandwiches.

The only ingredient needed to make labaney is laban (p. 147).

PREPARE THE LABANEY

~ Pour 2 quarts laban into a tightly woven unbleached muslin cloth which has been placed over a strainer.

~ When the whey or liquid is drained into the bowl over which the strainer is placed, the labaney has the consistency of a creamy spread.

~ Serve the labaney.

~ Put in a container (I prefer glass) and add a little olive oil on top of the labaney.

MAKES: about 2 cups.

JIBNEY (Cheese)

A cheese gentle to the palate, served at breakfast, also as an appetizer salted to taste.

1 gallon whole milk
4-5 junket rennet tablets
½ teaspoon salt

~ Heat milk to lukewarm temperature.

~ Using a little cold milk, dissolve the junket tablets well, mix these with the warm milk and stir well for about 3 minutes.

~ Cover for about 1 hour until the milk is firm.

~ Stir again a little until the whey separates from cheese and leave alone for 10 to 15 minutes. If whey does not separate well, heat the milk again until the whey separates.

~ Cover large strainer with cheese cloth. Put the cheese mixture into it and cover with the cloth.

~ After whey has drained, add salt on top of the cheese and refrigerate until cheese is firm enough to slice cleanly.

~ Cut into large pieces, add a little salt again if you wish. Keep refrigerated.

TIME: 1½ hours.   MAKES: 5 large pieces.

PART THREE

MORE FOOD FOR THOUGHT
from
Nathra Nader

While at college and graduate school we used to find some pleasurable moments in reading selections of "sayings" or "quotations," including Bartlett's volume. It very gradually dawned on us that often the insights which came from our parents were more to the point and fuller of meaning than the highly touted but disembodied contributions of the *literati*.

Much of this preference was due no doubt to a context for their observations that was more familiar to us; but there seemed to be a broader appeal to them beyond the family. So all four children began collecting our parents' thoughts and pithy responses and, as the years passed, we added to our compilation from relatives and friends who retained fond recollections. We were further encouraged by several reporters and writers who had met and spoken with our parents.

The following pages recount some of our father's contributions to this oral tradition at his home and restaurant. Dad had an ironic twist to many of his comments and he had his own version of the Socratic method with his children. He put in long hours in his restaurant, but he was not going to let business get in the way of speaking out. That, after all, was one reason he emigrated to the United States in 1912, at the age of nineteen. Sometimes he lost business because of his opinions, but he always said it was a cheap price to pay, adding on several occasions: "When I sailed past the Statue of Liberty, I took it seriously." Early on, he reflected a belief that Bertrand Russell once expressed: "It is clear that thought is not free if the profession of certain opinions makes it impossible to earn a living." For Dad, the restaurant especially was both a place to eat and a place to talk about community and other public issues. People used to say: "At Nader's place, for a nickel you got a cup of coffee and ten minutes of conversation."

There was also lively conversation around the dinner table at home, with or without guests. He believed in questions which helped us to remember what was said. He enjoyed making us think about the broader moral content of certain words which long ago had been debased by politicians or merchants. "Wealth" was one of his favorite topics. "The wealth of a society," he would say, "should create happiness for all the people, not misery to the many for the benefit of the few." He defined wealth to mean more than money or belongings; health was wealth, legacies to future generations were wealth, happiness was wealth, and the right to achieve justice was a pre-eminent source of wealth in his mind. Our mother would elaborate these points of view with many illustrations.

Hypocrisy and pompousness were favorite subjects for his barbs, so naturally he gave considerable attention to politicians and other forms of organized phoniness. Particularly relishing was going after insatiable greed by big business and the professions, both of which he found relentless in their drive to control the law, government and the flow of clear information. He especially opposed what he viewed as the drive by giant chain stores to destroy family-owned small businesses.

Nonetheless, Dad genuinely felt sorry for rich people even as he trounced them. "They live in a gold cage," he would say, "their luxuries draping over nervous and empty lives that otherwise could contribute to the community's well-being."

Father was suspicious of people who make sure to overcomplicate matters, and some intellectuals were high on his list. Is there a teenage problem? Instead of endlessly psychoanalyzing their delinquencies, simply recognize that youngsters need to be wanted, guided and usefully occupied. Then, get on with applying those venerable truisms in a variety of family and neighborhood ways.

Well, enough foreshadowing, let Dad, his sayings and their settings speak for themselves.

The Children

SAYINGS AND SETTINGS

Your best teacher is your last mistake, no tuition required.

Setting: Said often to the children whenever they would moan and groan about something they did poorly or in error.

It's been said that we are still governed by the documents and institutions of people long dead. Sometimes when I look at what's alive, I'm not worried.

Setting: Said at a dinner discussion during which one child complained about the heavy hand of the past.

If you don't use your rights, you'll lose your rights.

Setting: A family discussion on how the New England town meeting was being abandoned or weakened by numerous local governments.

The biggest single difference between the oppressors of history and their many victims is organization.

Setting: Observed at a family discussion about why so few have been able to brutalize so many throughout history.

So often in history, people who think with their minds take their cues from people who act with their feet.

Setting: Said during the Sixties when law professors and law students began to defend victims of civil rights abuses and urban poverty after protest marches, beatings and riots.

Reformers are too often satisfied with the passage of a law and the establishment of its program. These are just tools, not results. Moving to

results is much more difficult. The reformers are on to other matters while the rascals stay put.

Setting: During a family exchange over why good laws often make little difference in practice.

We make a mistake whenever we confuse schooling with intelligence. I've seen an insurance salesman who never finished high school take a Ph.D. to the cleaners with a sales pitch that a hog farmer would have seen through in a flash.

Setting: Said in reply to a comment by a child, home from college, describing the shopping habits of some classmates.

There should be a dictionary of hypocrisy and hypocrites that comes out every year. That way, as each yearly edition gets thicker, we can better know what's happening to our society.

Setting: Said during conversation about government euphemisms such as "cost growth," "revenue enhancement," "defoliation," and the one that set off his absurdity bell: a "unidirectional impact generator" to describe simple $10 claw hammers which a military contractor sold to the Pentagon for $450 each.

Watch out that your way of opposing your worst adversaries does not make you more like them. For if that happens, they've won.

Setting: Remarked to his son who was helping out in the restaurant, after hearing some customers arguing that anything goes if you want to win.

Congress is the best big business investment in the country. It's one big leveraged sell-out.

Setting: Asserted while watching a news analysis on Congress being unlikely to do anything about a wave of corporate mergers.

Colleges now teach students how to make a living instead of how to make a life.

Setting: Upon hearing a discussion by students talking excitedly about taking only courses that would land them a good paying job. Our parents did not send their children to college for career training.

Don't look down on anyone and don't be in awe of anyone.

Setting: Responding to his daughter, while walking home one day, who saw a street cleaner and said how glad she was not to be a street cleaner. He said she should respect street cleaners if only because they are doing work that she did not want to do but needed to be done. He ended with the above-noted remark.

They are cursed by neither poverty nor riches.

Setting: Spoken during a dinner-time exchange over who is happier on the whole, the poor, the middle class or the rich. He was always interested in what brought people happiness, refusing to accept the notion that money was the major way to a good life.

The coming of tyranny builds like a coral reef, bit by bit, quietly until the democratic ship runs aground against it and then the passengers cry out "what happened?"

Setting: In reaction to the McCarthyite red-baiting of the early Fifties when he would hear people shrug it off as unworrisome. He understood the power of incremental damage.

Almost everyone will claim they love their country. If that is true, why don't they spend more time improving it?

Setting: During a lively exchange with customers over coffee in the restaurant. For him patriotism of words had to be accompanied by deeds.

If the government (in Washington) is so opposed to communism, why does it work overtime fertilizing so much ground for communism overseas? When is Washington ever going to side with the peasants?

Setting: Commenting on the government's support over the years of dictatorships in the Third World.

The mindless "we're first" mentality in America can be taken too far. It has gotten in the way of learning from other nations and cultures and makes us less likely to be sensitive to areas of life where we are neither first, nor second, nor third.

Setting: Observed in reaction to politicians repeating the "America is Number One" theme before elections while opposing measures to provide health insurance to Americans and to reduce infant mortality.

This exchange with a Doctor having a ten cent cup of coffee in the restaurant around 1957:

Dr: Why are the auto workers' wages so high?

NN: So they can afford to pay your bills.

NN: Why do your charge so much?

Dr: Because we often treat poor people free.

NN: Well in that case, (smiling) since we give free coffee to poor people, your coffee today is $1.00. Thank you.

We will not have lasting peace in the world until we settle the differences between greed and need, greed for excessive power and money and the need for necessary power and money.

Setting: A favorite reminder anytime people believed that diplomatic deals or military prowess by themselves would bring stability.

Bureaucracy is what organizations in all countries have in common with one another; bureaucracy is the seeming drug of choice for government, large businesses and labor unions.

Setting: Commenting on one of the most common complaints (more and more red tape) customers spoke about in the restaurant.

Socialism is government ownership of the means of production, while capitalism is business ownership of the means of government.

Setting: Reacting to a news article in the early Fifties about graft and special favors in Washington to the wealthy and powerful commercial interests.

Capitalism is the freest economic system if only we can control it. Capitalism will always survive in the U.S. as long as the government is willing to use socialism (your taxes) to bail it out.

Setting: Noted with irony during a little debate between customers in the restaurant shortly before World War II about which system is better.

Why are you insulting your parents?

Setting: Chiding nonplussed teenagers who, while waiting to be served in the restaurant, mischievously poured pepper in a sugar bowl.

Every time I hear someone say "dumb animal," I have to laugh. "Dumb animals" do not smoke or drink, they don't kill their own, they don't wage organized war, they don't soil their own nest and they don't watch television when they eat ... otherwise they're stupid.

Setting: Said to his son after they walked past some urchins who were verbally harassing a hapless neighborhood dog.

Sloth of mind and body is the greatest power on earth, if we define power as that which causes more things to happen or not happen because of it.

Setting: Expressed during a dinner conversation in which he challenged the children to give examples of the laziest behavior they could imagine.

Something is very wrong in any government where the easiest way to lose your job is to do your job.

Setting: A comment on hearing about a conference one of his children was holding on ethical government whistleblowers.

When the rich get our tax money it's called a subsidy; when the poor get it, it's called welfare. Actually the rich are our biggest welfare cases.

Setting: Chuckling over Ronald Reagan's harping on the alleged welfare queen (a composite character as it were) in Chicago during his 1980 Presidential campaign.

Elections are like auctions. Politicians trot themselves out daily to give a piece of themselves in return for campaign money.

Setting: A frequent, seasonal commentary during election periods.

When politicians are engaged in bad deeds, they most often raise the flag and invoke God.

Setting: Noted during one of Richard Nixon's televised speeches.

People throughout history have responded more to leaders who have asked them to believe than to leaders who have asked them to think. Once again the power of sloth at work.

Setting: Remarks during a dinner table exchange on the fervor of mass movements over the centuries.

Well, what did you learn in school today? Did you learn to believe or did you learn to think?

Setting: Greeting his ten-year-old child one day coming home from school.

A necessary condition for the decline of any society is the widespread feeling among the people that "it can't happen here."

Setting: A regular reaction to anyone who boasts too much about our country's political superiority. He always thought that boasting breeds a dangerous complacency.

Separate a politician from his smile and you're halfway home to knowing what he is really up to.

Setting: Reflecting on Ronald Reagan's use of the political smile.

If anything is worse than being a miser, it is a generous person who refuses the generosity of others.

Setting: Describing a compassionate relative who always gave hospitality but was unwilling to receive any in return.

It is better to have religion without the church than a church without religion. Throughout history millions of people have died in the name of organized religion. The Gods must be most displeased by their followers doing all this killing in their names. Nowadays it is the business mentality that affects too many church ministries and what they are losing can be measured by the genuine contributions to justice made by other churches and clergy of conscience and social action. It would be helpful to many people if those clergy who most flaunt the Bible would on occasion apply it.

Setting: Delivered while watching the television preachers one Sunday.

Far more people know how to make big money than know how to spend their money in useful ways. After they pile it up they hardly know what to do with it, except spoil their descendants.

Setting: In response to a discussion of the stagnation or uselessness of dormant large fortunes.

The inequality of sacrifice in wartime is staggering. In World War II, young Americans who had most to live for were the quickest to die, while businessmen made huge profits back home. Inequality was inevitable given the age difference, but it did not have to be that great a difference. In wartime, companies which profit from war should be required to give something back to the veterans who survive.

Setting: Saddened by the plight of injured veterans coming home from the war, he wanted the war industries to use some of their large profits to help these men, and not leave such help entirely up to the government. The help he urged was not just money but using their influence in many directions.

Handling success is more difficult than achieving it. Just look at the lives of the very rich and unhappy celebrities.

Setting: Both our parents would remind us of this maxim whenever we would hear the stories of Hollywood personalities or star athletes falling apart.

A great thinker who writes incomprehensibly needs to do more thinking. Really great thinkers write with great clarity unless they are just writing messages to themselves.

Setting: Consoling one of his children in college, who thought it was her fault that she could not understand some turgid 19th century philosopher.

Would you rather have a chance without a choice or a choice without a chance?

Setting: A typical puzzle question directed at the children to stimulate a wide-ranging discussion about social conditions and their impact on individuals.

People need to think their way out of poverty before they can work their way out of poverty, assuming they are able-bodied and not ill. The work follows the motivation of the thought. Ambition, timing, tactics, determination are all thoughts that give work an escalator.

Setting: During a family conversation on why among similarly situated poor people, some make it out of poverty and others do not, though both work hard.

There is an Arabic proverb that says: "If you are going to lie, be sure you have a good memory."

Setting: An indelible remark to one child after father observed that a restaurant supplier was not leveling with him based on what that supplier had put in writing to him a year earlier.

Most politicians would rather be flattered than remembered. In politics, unfortunately, the same is true for a sizable number of voters. This combination of mutual flattery is very bad for democracy and elections.

Setting: Watching a national political convention on television that was steeped in long-winded flattery.

The only thing the Democratic candidates have in common is that they're all alike. The Republicans might as well run corporations for elected office. At least that would get them down to their basics.

Setting: Comment on a state election and on the existing party system.

Whenever we judge business, we should ask: Do these companies just seek temporary wealth for themselves or genuine wealth for society? I see far more of the former in today's big businesses than earlier in the century, more creation of temporary paper wealth without building up the nation's basic productivity.

Setting: Reflecting on the news about all the funny money deals and mergers during the Seventies.

Popular revolutions so often fail because the people are not ready for the day after. Revolutions for the peoples' benefit are more than a rejection of evil and other injustices. They are an invitation for people to govern themselves. That is the hardest work and if it is not treated seriously, all that happens after the victory parades are over is too often the replacement of old despots with new despots.

Setting: During family dinner talk about history. He was not one for empty political slogans.

What is the true value of ethnic identity? Culture, humor, variety and a common sociability for facing life. But for politics, humanity should replace ethnicity.

Setting: Recalling ethnic tensions in Newark where he once owned a small grocery store in the early Twenties.

Have you heard the oil companies say how it is their oil and gas in the ground? I was not aware that Standard Oil was around millions of years ago to make oil and gas out of rotting vegetation. "But we found it," say the oil companies. So did the explorers claim to have "found" the Mississippi River, but they didn't get to keep it.

Setting: Observation during the energy crisis of the early Seventies.

Big changes often come from small changes that add up day after day. Wear a sweater when cold and replace a bit of heating oil company sales. Eat wisely and weaken the junk food hold of the food companies. Walk and exercise and don't abuse yourself with smoke and drink and you'll reduce the bills of doctors and hospitals. When we don't take care of ourselves and think for ourselves, we are producing the inventories for business.

Setting: Part of a conversation about the amazing spread of the non-smoking movement.

Businesses that refuse to change their harmful or wasteful ways use a great deal of influence getting governments to devise problems that block out old solutions.

Setting: Stated when the Carter government launched the expensive synfuel subsidy programs instead of backing faster energy conservation approaches nationwide.

It is a rare combination to find a strong sense of justice matched by an equally strong abhorrence of violence.

Setting: Commenting on Mahatma Ghandi's activities against the British occupation of India.

Genuine patriotism is being pleased with how far our country has come and displeased with how far we have yet to go.

Setting: Frequent response to the viewpoints summed up in the "America, right or wrong," and "America, love it or leave it" slogans.

"Wisdom" and "thrifty" are words I heard used a great deal years ago. But I hardly ever hear them anymore. Maybe the rejection of the experience of older people and the onrushing wasteful economy may have much to do with the retirement of these words.

Setting: Father grew up "recycling" almost everything possible to reuse from clothes to string to paper. And his elders were seen as valuable sources of advice and insight. Not anymore, he noted in the Sixties. But maybe both recycling and learning from elders are making a comeback.

Business with too much political power over government seeks special treatment, protection from competition, subsidies, leniency from good laws. The more business succeeds in this way, the flabbier and more reckless it will become. Then everybody will suffer -- workers, consumers, taxpayers, health, safety and the productiveness of the economy.

Setting: Expressed following a news dispatch about the troubles and inefficiency of the steel industry in the early Seventies.

Unions talk about higher wages but almost never about higher prices except as a way to push for higher wages. This is a way of placing their workers on a treadmill, not to mention the effect on the larger number of poorer workers. It is also a way to avoid dealing with many basic economic injustices at the root which sooner or later will plague the condition of all workers. Unions have adjusted to the power of big business instead of challenging its grip on so much of our society and other societies abroad.

Setting: Making a point at dinner on why unions were no match for business.

Your Senators, Representatives and President in Washington spend over 20 percent of your income, which requires you to work over 2 months a year to supply them with those taxes. How much money and time do you spend each year watching how they spend your dollars?

Setting: Conversation with a group of customers sitting around the counter complaining about the mess in Washington. He gave them a free round of coffee for their taking this gibe so well.

Foresight is often a decision which pinches now but pleases later.

Setting: Said to one of his children coming from school after a history lesson where the purchase of Alaska (then called "Seward's Folly") was discussed.

A society is in trouble when its problems become more profitable than its solutions and its questions far more numerous than its answers. An economy loses its quality when waste is built in as a regular way to profits. Vehicles are built to waste fuel. There are more throwaway consumer goods. Even thrift is seen as un-American by the advertising industry.

Setting: During a wide-ranging family talk about how all kinds of shoddiness generate more economic sales but damage the economy's quality.

Economies start out responding to needs, then expand to wants, then to frivolities. Guess where the American economy is coming from and heading toward?

Setting: While watching a televised news program on the booming economy for some and the millions in need who are left behind. Plenty of games in the stores but not enough housing or health care, he added.

People aren't as likely to spend money to save money as they are likely to spend money to make money. They're missing out on an indirect raise in pay when they don't shop wisely.

Setting: Explaining to the children why not buying quality in products can cost more in repairs and replacements. Today, the modern phrase is "life cycle costing."

A politician once said to me "You have to do things you don't believe in order to win elective office so you then can do the things you do believe in." Can you believe that?

Setting: Dad used to slow down political candidates, who rushed along the long restaurant counter shaking hands, in order to engage them in some talk. His approach was to hold on to their handshake until he said his piece and got an answer. The above was one such answer.

How can you tell a phony politician right off? When he is shaking your hand, looking toward the next person to greet, not listening to what you are saying, all the while flattering you.

Setting: One of his many amusing descriptions of politicians who "worked" the counter and tables at the restaurant.

When I passed the Statue of Liberty in 1912 I took it seriously.

Setting: In reply to a less than friendly customer in the restaurant who said: "How do you expect to make a profit and deliver your controversial opinions every day?"

When asked whether I am a Republican or a Democrat, I reply that I am an American.

Setting: His distaste for the two Parties' shenanigans and posturing was extensive and often laced with humor. He believed that more and more they were representing the same powerful interests. He once brought a lawsuit in federal court against the Democratic Party in Connecticut to allow independent voters to vote in the primary since taxpayers were paying for the event. Although he lost the case, a later case brought by then-Senator Lowell Weicker did advance the principle he was espousing.

Any political movement that is dull is doomed. It also helps to have its name be just one word. The longer the name, the less attention it is likely to receive.

Setting. Reflecting on utopians' detailed plans for utopia.

You can be a slave if you do not have a dollar and another kind of slave if you have too many dollars.

Setting: Reply to a young salesman telling Dad how rich he wants to be.

Television has replaced the dictator's ban on three or more people gathering in public without a permit.

Setting: Replying to his wife's observation on how few people were chatting anymore on the town's Main Street sidewalks in the late Fifties.

I'd rather have a leader who is only as strong as the cause than a cause which is only as strong as the leader.

Setting: Dinner table talk about charismatic leaders who were long on oratory and short on substance.

There have been too many revolutions against external domination that have resulted in the seizure of power by internal groups bent on internal domination.

Setting: A frequent comment on headlines regarding various revolutions with fine-sounding slogans that leave bitter aftertastes.

How often national politicians wrap the Bible and the Flag around their behavior while disgracing both.

Setting: While listening to a comparison of a president's slogans with his deeds.

Proverbs helped to bring up the children; they advise, admonish and warm their minds. Arabic is a language rich in proverbs. Although the following proverbs do not translate with the rhyme and context of the originals, here are some father and mother applied to us:

- *To a child talking silly:* "Jokes are to words as salt is to taste" meaning, don't overdo it.

- *To a child delaying:* "Wait oh, mule, until the grass grows up."

- *To a child showing off:* "The more that you exceed, the more that you subtract."

- *To a child who is talking more than listening:* "You have two ears and one mouth, so at least listen twice as much as you talk."

- *To a child not showing respect for an older sibling:* "A day older is a year wiser."

- *To a child who was prone to mumbling, a father original:* "You'll never grow hungry." The child asks, why? "Because if you have no food, you'll eat your words!"

"New" has become an all-purpose word for "better." Sometimes new is better but sometimes new is worse. Just ask yourself why does everything called progress have to be new? The best parts and structures of the world's great cities were set generations ago, London, Paris, Washington. Just because advertisers try to make us buy their products by labelling them "new," doesn't mean we should be so accepting. We are losing much old knowledge and wisdom because they are not "new."

Setting: Said at a pre-dinner social with a family visiting us accompanied by their young children who, their parents said, kept clamoring for them to buy the latest "new" toys.

This country has an insufficient supply of intellectuals who are educated, sure to be a drain on the future.

Setting: Dad always wondered why those who think for a living made such a small contribution to finding solutions for what should be solvable problems, large and small, in society. What appalled him was the available supply of ingenious minds developing ever more destructive weapon systems and how few ingenious minds were working on how to wage peace or eradicate poverty.

A middle-class standard of living nowadays usually means two family breadwinners taking on a high consumer debt and mortgage, showing a low net worth and spending too little time with the children.

Setting: Asserted during the early Eighties when recalling that in the Fifties one working class breadwinner in our state could buy a modest house and a car.

The greatest obstacle to good government in a democracy is the feeling by too many citizens that they just don't count.

Setting: His customary reply to anyone who gave him the shrugged shoulder, "ah, what's the use, you can't fight city hall" routine.

There are politicians who bore and those who flatter and those who agitate and those who inspire and those who involve and serve the people and those who are smoothies and those who steal and those who love the limelight and those who are empire-builders and those who are lazy and those who are in someone's pocket and those who are just plain dim.

Setting: Recounted while trying to get the children thinking in terms of different kinds of politicians and not an all-inclusive image.

A corrupt politician damages twice. He weakens the public trust for his own enrichment and discourages good people from going into politics because they think it's too dirty.

Setting: Reacting to a news story about corruption in Boston.

For the local community, I'll take independent businesses over national chain stores. They are more committed to the town because they are where they are, rooted there. The small business in town contributes to local charities and can't pass the buck to some national headquarters. More often they are involved in community organizations, while chain managers are frequently transferred. They disperse power rather than concentrate it. They don't have such rigid rules for their customers. Judgment and discretion are more possible in contrast to the "that's company policy, I only work here" attitude of chain employees. They certainly provide more opportunity for family self-employment and overall more diversity than the standardized chain that is the same in Los Angeles as it is in West Hartford, Connecticut. They cannot drive other businesses out of business by swinging their weight to cut prices in one area, until their competition is no more, and make it up in other areas. Chain managers are often under strong pressures by their bosses to meet sales and profit quotas and I've seen how in the supermarket business this can lead to cheating customers. Recently, chains are leading in separating consumers from closer contact with prices on their products and other automated conditions that become controlling forces on buyers by the managers.

Setting: Dad looked askance at chains. He thought there were many undesirable consequences over time to their replacing the retail family business in America, affecting neighborhoods, local opportunity to start new businesses and local self-reliance. To those who supported chains in the Thirties and Forties, when the topic of chain store power was a hot topic especially in small towns, and said that the prices were cheaper,

Dad would reply, "Wait until you see the prices when there is no longer any small business competition ... and wait until you see what is sold on the shelves." He used to remind his children that, during the Depression, poorer families could get food on credit from the corner grocery but never from the A&P supermarket chain in town.

Beware of victims or their descendants who become masters. Like the battered child becoming the beating adult, it can lead to a cycle of violence and self-destruction.

Setting: Discussing the tragic ironies of history at the dinner table.

Any country that rejects or abuses its truthsayers is sure eventually to turn them into prophets.

Setting: Expressed in an exchange about ethical whistleblowers exposing corruption and crimes in government and business.

Unless you know all the answers, why don't you have any questions?

Setting: Said to the children when they remained quiet after he had challenged them on some issue at the dinner table.

In our society, people are grown old rather than grow old.

Setting: Speaking with his daughter who told him that the 94-year-old, famous reporter George Seldes, wanted to write a book titled, *To Hell with Old Age* as a protest against the aging "industry" which seeks to program older adults for a mind-numbing "comfortable retirement."

The only time I believed the Democrats is when they spoke about the Republicans and the only time I believed the Republicans is when they spoke about the Democrats. Now I'm not so sure even about that.

Setting: Said partly tongue-in-cheek to two partisan customers, one a Republican and the other a Democrat, who were having their regular breakfast in the restaurant.

One reason why so few educators pay attention to the quality of education for our children is that quality doesn't cost enough.

Setting: Dad's ironic twist in pointing out that money and buildings do not produce quality in the schools; only deep care about the children does.

First, let's corrupt the language; that'll give us more time, aye?

Setting: Packing off to bed two of his children who were using evasive language to justify staying up later that night.

Don't separate your mind from your brain or let anyone else do that for you.

Setting: A caution conveyed to the children whenever anyone of them was acting up.

Whenever anyone criticizes our country or its government publicly, there is always somebody who says "if you don't like it, leave it." But, that is one reason so many immigrants came to this country because, unlike where they were, they could stay and try to improve the situation.

Setting: One could always see the gleam of the anticipation in Dad's eyes when ho saw this "love it or leave it" routine coming.

One way to look at government's performance is first to look at ourselves in the mirror. Maybe then we may see that the reason why our government is not up to our standards is because we have not been up to our own citizen standards in making it work for us.

Setting: Remarked in a broad-ranging dinner discussion with the children and some of their visiting classmates on what does and does not lead to good government.

"Don't you think we'd love to have you visit us?" She replied, " yes of course." "Then why are you so miserly with your presence," he rejoined.

Setting: Said at age 96, during a long-distance call to a younger cousin.

As a society, we don't use doctors wisely. If we used them to protect us from sickness, instead of only calling them when we're sick, medicine would have a better reputation. How many doctors are practicing full-time to get people to stop smoking or drinking heavily or eating bad food compared to the number of doctors operating or prescribing medicines? Our system doesn't pay for prevention; after leaving many poor people outside, it pays for sickness.

Setting: One of his frequent comments on preventive medicine being subordinated to more profitable medicine.

The best tax is one that is fair, simple, easy to collect, and difficult to avoid. To me that means a progressive sales tax with safeguards for the poor and higher rates on luxurious goods and harmful or addictive products like tobacco. The income tax has become too complex, too full of special exceptions, too influential on business and even savings decisions and too good for bookkeepers, accountants and lawyers who make us dependent on them as they feed off the complexities. Look at a bottle of whiskey or gin and see the stamp tax on it, simple, easy to collect and difficult to avoid.

Setting: Conveyed during a family conversation on what the best tax system would be like. When the point was raised about the rich possibly getting richer without any income tax, Dad delivered his favorite, idealistic solution to self-perpetuating greed and the wealthy's overall lack of community contributions as follows:

If a society truly wants to achieve economic justice and still keep incentives for economic activity, the limitation of wealth with unlimited income should be considered by a popular referendum, after much debate. The ceiling on individual wealth, if it is not spent or given away, would be enforced by a wealth tax, say above a million dollars in net worth per person with a reasonable homestead exemption.

In this way the wealthy would become more interested in donating their money to community betterment (after all, how much can they consume?) or spreading the wealth among more people. The present system now makes a bad joke of progressive income taxation. But, a tax on wealth, not on income, plus a progressive sales tax would stop the endless greed to accumulate wealth and redirect the motivations toward community generosity. Either we spread the wealth in this world, where billions of humans go without, or we spread the misery.

Setting: Repeatedly, in discussions about the future in the restaurant, social gatherings or with the family, Dad would impress this view "*if* we want a better life for everybody." He would point out the example of a large clock manufacturer in our home town who built and endowed a high school and a large home for orphans. Limitations of wealth with unlimited income, he argued, would provide incentive for such contributions and soon they would become traditions. There would follow more local reliance, a warmer feeling between people and no more inheritance of great wealth by children and grandchildren who become spoiled as a result.

Long ago, he realized that economies with more equitable distribution of wealth were far more prosperous economies with far bigger markets. His favorite example was an agricultural economy with many small farmers in contrast to one dominated by huge plantations. He hoped that the practical difficulties in adopting the limited wealth, unlimited income proposal would be overcome once enough people realized all the benefits that would follow and the anguish and anxiety that would be avoided.

Conclusion

In 1978 at the age of 86, Dad led a demonstration of townspeople up Main Street to protest a Congressional Pay Raise. He has always believed that public officials should possess a capacity for shame and that neither their performance nor their needs required such higher pay while the government was running in red ink and turning its back on the people. A wire service sent the photo of the demonstration around the country.